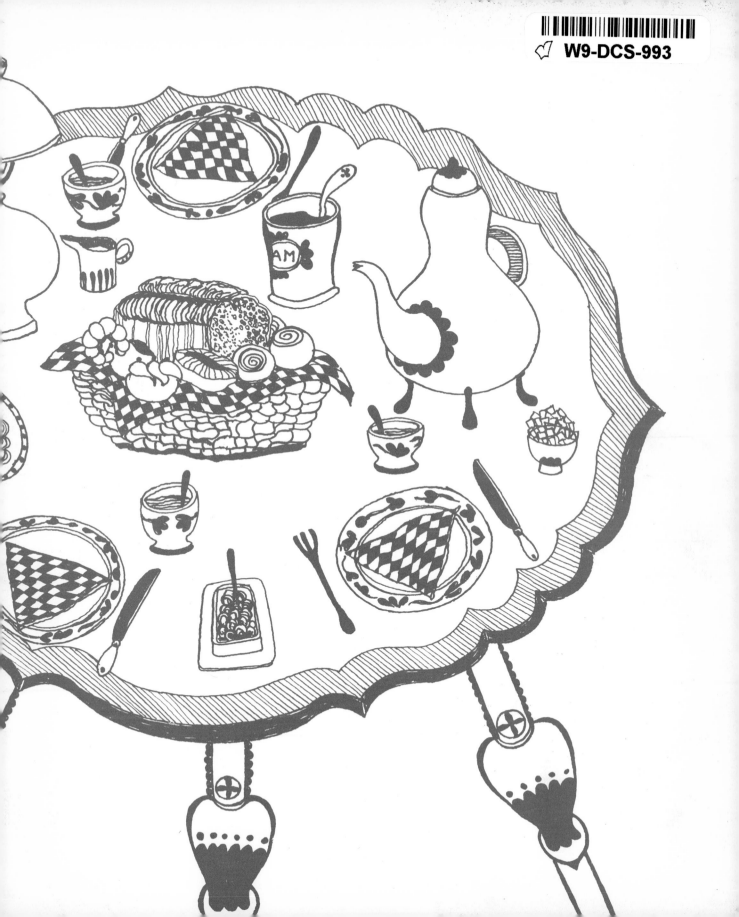

'Round the world cooking library
Dutch and Belgian Cooking

Traditional dishes from the low countries

Recipe contributions

by Heleen A. M. Halverhout

author of 'The Netherlands Cookbook'

GALAHAD BOOKS • NEW YORK

Contents

Recipe contributions	Heleen A. M. Halverhout, author of 'The Netherlands Cookbook' and many other cookbooks, Amsterdam
American editor	Irena Kirshman, graduate Cordon Bleu Cooking School, lecturer on international cuisines, food consultant, New York, N.Y.
Associate American editor	Susan Wright, New York, N.Y.

Editorial staff for 'Round the world cooking library

Project editor	Wina Born, Dame de la Chaîne des Rôtisseurs and member of the board of the Fédération Internationale de la Presse Gastronomique
Executive editor	Ton van Es
Text editor U.S.A.	Martin Self B.A.,J.D.
Cover photo	Henk van der Heijden, Amsterdam
Text photos	Bob Ris, Studio Meijer Pers B.V., Amsterdam
Design and drawings	Rosemarijn van Limburg Stirum, Amsterdam
Created by	Meijer Pers B.V., Amsterdam, The Netherlands
Typeset by	Service Type Inc., Lancaster, Pennsylvania and Internationaal Zetcentrum B.V., Wormerveer, The Netherlands
Printed by	Drukkerij Meijer B.V., Wormerveer, The Netherlands
Bound by	Proost en Brandt N.V., Amsterdam, The Netherlands
Publisher	Drake Publishers Inc., New York, N.Y.
Distributor	Galahad books, New York, N.Y.

Cup measures in this book are based on an eight ounce cup.

Holland and Belgium at the table

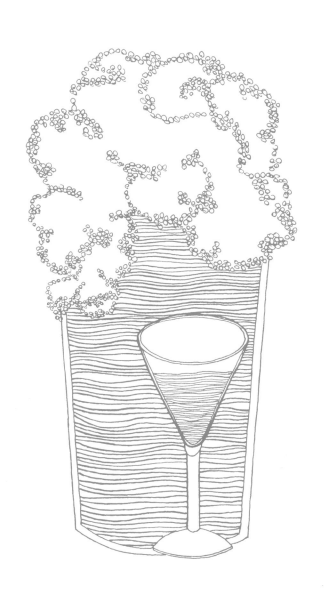

The Netherlands and Belgium, two small countries, lie together on the west coast of continental Europe near the mouth of the Rhine. Together with neighboring Luxembourg they form the free-trade area called simply Benelux. Foreigners sometimes hardly distinguish between these countries, but the differences between the Netherlands and Belgium are in fact very great. The Dutchman seems careful, thrifty and home-loving; the Belgian appears more easy-going and fond of a night out. Certainly a good example of this difference in national character is that the Belgians drink at least ten times as much champagne as the Dutch, though champagne costs the same in both countries. This difference is also reflected in cooking. Dutch food is substantial, simple and straightforward; Belgian food is richer and more like French cuisine – lavish and full of imagination.

The Dutch have always had to struggle against Nature, and above all against the sea. Large parts of the Netherlands have been reclaimed from the sea over centuries, and the task still goes on. To keep this land which lies below sea level dry and arable, it must be drained continuously, using dikes. Some of the new polderland, now being turned into rich farms, lies 15 feet below sea level. In earlier times the level of the water was controlled by windmills, still so characteristic of Holland. Today it is done with electric hydraulic pumps. Dutch children also learn to cope with the struggle against nature very early in life, especially when they have to bicycle along one of the polder roads for half an hour against the wind and rain to be on time for school.

No wonder, then, that they carry a few thick cheese sandwiches in their school bags; nothing creates as much of an appetite as bicycling — particularly against the wind. The lush grass that grows in the damp polders gives the black-and-white Dutch cows a glossy and well-cared-for look. The creamy milk these animals yield goes into the famous Dutch cheeses: round, orange-yellow Edam, light-yellow Gouda, in the form of a large, flat wheel, and the less well known cheese from Leiden, seasoned with cumin seeds.

Once, cheese was made on every farm. Now, only in the province of South Holland are there still cheesemaking country women who have velvety-soft hands from kneading curdled milk and who know the secret of making golden-yellow, creamy and full-flavored Gouda. The cheese these women make is marked 'country cheese' and sold at the market in the medieval town of Gouda.

In a country that has so much

A Dutch polder is below sea level surrounded by dikes. Windmills pump away the excess water from this flat and lush land where drainage ditches are the only fences needed for the sleek black and white cows.

An old mustard mill in the region of Amsterdam where food industries have flourished since the 16th century.

Dutch fish preserves: sour herring in pots, smoked herring ('bokking') in wooden crates.

The medieval herb gardens in Leiden, where medicinal herbs for the famous medical school of the University of Leiden were cultivated.

water surrounding it and so many rivers, lakes and canals, it goes without saying that fish dishes are popular. The Netherlands are especially famous for two unique fish delicacies: herring which come from the sea, and eel, which come from inland waters. In the fifteenth century a Dutchman made an important discovery about herring gutting and curing: as soon as the herrings are caught and brought on board the fishing boats, they are cleaned, but a particular gland is left in the fish. Because of this, the herrings obtain a unique flavor after being salted and stored in wooden barrels. Herrings prepared in this way on fishing boats are called 'maatjes' herrings (from the word 'maagde' or virgins, because the fish are still so young that they have not yet formed a roe). In Holland, these fresh, young and fat herrings are usually called 'new herrings'. The day before the herring fleets first set sail in May is a festive occasion, and the gaily decorated boats parade along the coast. The next day, the race begins for the first catch. The season's first barrel of herring, in a grand, traditional cask, is always presented to the Queen. In the streets of many cities of Holland, there are still small herring stalls, decked with the Dutch flag and surrounded by crowds at the beginning of the season. Here, the way to eat is

6

to take one of these soft, oyster-flavored fishes by the tail, throw your head back and let the fish slide down your throat. In the small picturesque towns along the coast, fat eels from the IJsselmeer are smoked until soft and golden. They are served warm on toasted bread as hors d'oeuvres.

The Dutch begin the day with a substantial breakfast to ready themselves for the chilling rain, strong wind, wet snow storms or whatever else the whimsical Dutch climate at its worst can surprise them with.

Old-fashioned farmers have a bowl of warm porridge with plenty of sugar, hot pancakes, or thick sandwiches with cheese and fried bacon. After this

comes a sandwich with molasses.

The ideal Dutch breakfast in town consists of tea, sometimes milk, a soft-boiled egg, cheese, often ham or smoked meat, jam and different sorts of bread, including a slice of currant bread spread with butter. For most Dutchmen, however, this is a Sunday breakfast, but hotels serve a meal like this to their guests every morning.

At half past ten, the ritual 'cup of coffee' is served everywhere: at home, at the office, in shops or on the job. On trains, the waiter walks through the cars selling coffee. Housewives go to their neighbors for a cup of coffee and a chat. The large cup of coffee, with sugar and warm

milk, is usually served with cookies, and if it is someone's birthday, he treats everyone to cakes and pastries—even at the office.

Lunch is served at about half past twelve. In Holland it is called, inevitably, 'coffee time.' The so-called 'coffee table' consists of all sorts of bread, coffee and milk, sausages, ham or other cold cuts, cheeses, jam and fruit. If there are guests for lunch, they are served a cup of soup, sandwiches, salads such as herring salad and Russian salad, or some hot dish such as an omelet, or scrambled eggs. But the open sandwich remains the central course of this meal. Tea time is at four o'clock (when cakes and cookies appear at the

table), and at five o'clock the Dutch begin to look forward to the 'borrel' (or cocktail), a small glass of the national drink, 'genever', or Dutch gin. There are two types, 'old' and 'young', but the difference between the two is not in age, but in taste, aroma and color. Old genever is light-yellow and has a rather strong taste and aroma; young genever is white and has a neutral taste. Genever has always been a man's drink. In Holland, men always drink it at the end of the day, standing at the bar of an old café where it is warm, smoky and comfortable, with the furnishings a bit old and worn. Men come together in this club-like atmosphere to relax for

an hour, and then go home to the substantial, simple, evening meal which is so dear to the Dutch.

This begins with a tasty soup, preferably with meatballs and plenty of fresh vegetables, then a serving of potatoes and more fresh vegetables (often boiled or stewed) and the salad or apple sauce and a medium-sized piece of meat or fish. After this, the meal is ended with a pudding or custard made of stewed fruit or sweet rice cooked in milk—this is 'to fill up the holes,' as the Dutch say.

The patriarchal tradition of genever drinking is beginning to weaken, however. Young wives do not enjoy the fact that while they are in the kitchen cooking, their husbands are relaxing in the café. The man's glass of genever is increasingly taking second place to the unisex sherry that is now the universal apéritif in Holland. Husband and wife take a glass of sherry together at home, frequently with a piece of cheese. After conferences at the office, it is also becoming common to end the day with a glass of sherry.

Although calorie counting has spread to Holland, the Dutch remain attached to their traditional and filling winter dishes, such as pea soup and hodgepodge (potatoes and cabbage with sausages; recipes on page 43). During the winter, pea soup can be ordered in most any Dutch restaurant, snack-bar or café, in train stations or in factory canteens. Younger people, however, have become more cosmopolitan, and are trying Spanish, French, Italian and other foreign cuisines.

Dutch cooking is also becoming increasingly international. This is partly due to the traditional Dutch ties with the East, particularly with Indonesia, which was long a Dutch colony. Some Indonesian or Chinese recipes such as nassi goreng or bahmi, have become almost 'national' dishes. Indonesian or Chinese food is eaten frequently in many households, and even in small villages there are inexpensive Eastern restaurants that are always busy.

The Dutch also like to entertain guests in an untraditional manner. Fondue is often served to guests. Everyone sits at the table around a small pot filled with sizzling hot oil, in which small pieces of meat are cooked, and then eaten with many different sauces. This dish is probably of Far Eastern origin, but it has become particularly popular in the Netherlands. Another cosmopolitan fashion is not to invite friends to a cocktail party, but to a candlelit wine and cheese evening, with French wine, French cheese and French bread.

Although the traditionally homemade Dutch cheese is now most frequently produced in factories, there are still farmers, and especially farmers' wives, who make their own cheese on the farm. And any connoisseur knows that the cheeses made by these traditional country methods are worth their weight in gold. First of all, rennet is added to separate the curds from the whey. The curd (a vital part of the milk) must be 'cut' and then churned in wooden tubs. After the cheese has had a brine bath, it can ripen. Dutch country cheese can be bought in different stages of ripeness: young cheese, which is soft and creamy; old cheese, which is hearty, golden-yellow and full flavored; and aged cheese, which has become flaky and acquired a very special, somewhat piquant flavor.
The most famous Dutch cheese is Edam, a round cheese with a familiar red rind. In the picturesque old town of Alkmaar, every Friday during the summer you can see Edam cheese handled with great respect for tradition. Men in white suits, wearing straw hats with flowing ribbons, carry the cheese in barrows yoked on their shoulders. They jog along to the weighing house (an elaborate building with great scales where the cheeses are weighed). Probably the best loved cheese in Holland is the Gouda, a large, flat, round cheese which is still sold in the cheese market of Gouda, another picturesque old

town lying amidst the lush meadows that provide such excellent grazing for Holland's dairy herds.

The great 'herring holiday.' Just before the herring fleet sets sail around the end of May, a festive 'flag day' is celebrated. The ships are decorated and sail in parade along the coast. All of Holland anxiously awaits the first batch of this remarkable fish. Finally, when the newspaper headlines have announced 'New Herring Has Arrived', small herring stalls appear on the streets and all herring lovers rush out to try the New Herring to see if it is as good as it was the year before. The first batch is usually very expensive but real herring lovers gladly pay the price.

The Belgians are great lovers of the good life. This is apparent in the atmosphere created by one of the great Flemish painters of the 16th century, Pieter Bruegel, who excelled at painting country wedding feasts with red faced characters gleaming with pleasure, busily devouring juicy sausages and hams and drinking mugs of foamy beer. The Belgians are not only fond of eating plentifully, but also of eating well. They are almost as knowledgeable and critical of cooking as the French. This helps to explain the many exceptionally good restaurants in Belgium where the whole family goes on weekends. Belgium is also the home of the plump women who 'cook out' for families celebrating a birthday or a wedding. These women stay in the kitchen the whole day, rattling pots and pans and then bringing the most delicious things to the table. The northern part of Belgium, along the coast of the North Sea, is as flat, green and fertile as the Netherlands. And there are the same lush green polders on which sleek cattle graze. But Belgians raise cattle not so much for milk, butter and cheese as for meat; and the steaks that come from Flemish polders are among the best in the world. From the narrow dikes and canals come fat eels, eaten in a sauce of fresh green summer herbs found along the waterside.

The Belgians are famed for appreciating seafood. So much so, in fact, that large quantities of oysters, which come from Dutch waters, and mussels, which are caught along the Dutch coast, are exported to Belgium. Mussels are an important national dish in Belgium, eaten the year round with French fries and beer. The best place to have mussels is in the small popular restaurants where the owner's wife cooks them herself, sometimes on a large coal stove standing in the middle of the room. Tiny gray shrimp, which turn a beautiful soft red when cooked, are another Belgian speciality. In some places the shrimp are still caught as they were in the Middle Ages. Men sitting high on sturdy Flemish horses scoop the shrimp from the water with dip nets on the end of long poles and put their catch in two-wheeled horse carts. Every year in July, at the peak of the shrimp season, a shrimp feast is celebrated in honor of these sturdy fishermen, with a procession of them riding along the sea on horseback. The citizens of Ghent, the charming ancient Flemish city, are proud of a well known dish of their own, 'waterzooi,' a favorite of kings from Charles V in the 16th century to the present King Baudouin. Waterzooi consists of a plump chicken, cooked in water with vegetables and herbs and with a broth thickened with eggs and cream. True gourmets travel great distances to eat this dish at the charming Gothic halls of the St. Jorishof restaurant, built in the 13th century at Ghent. Afterwards, the best dessert is thick pancakes with plenty of butter and sugar.

Across the south of Belgium stretch the rugged hills of the Ardennes. This is a lonely land with a hard, wet climate. People say that when the door is open at the North Pole there is a draft in the Ardennes. But it is not only a land of extensive forests and marshy heaths, but also of clear small streams, well stocked with brook trout and exquisite summer crayfish. All the restaurants in the Ardennes have trout on the menu. The fish are often caught with a dip net from the brook behind the restaurant just before the meal and they are always accompanied at the table by delicious, slightly sparkling, light white wines from the sunny hills along the Moselle River in the small neighboring country of Luxembourg.

In the fall and winter, the Ardennes are a paradise for hunters and those who like game. Many restaurants, some situated in the middle of the woods in old mills or castles, organize a gastronomic weekend in the winter months. Gourmets from far and wide come to enjoy fabulous game dishes: wild boar, hare, pheasant and venison, that have been marinated for days in wine with cognac and herbs, and then braised with bacon and served with a compote of bilberries.

A very special ham also comes from the Ardennes: a ham smoked over a smouldering fire of juniper bush branches, with a particularly fragrant flavor. This rosewood-colored ham is usually sliced paper thin and accompanied by the light and dry white wine from Luxembourg and dark-brown country bread.

Driving through the small villages and towns of the

A familiar scene in all the villages and small towns of Belgium. Small terraces with wicker armchairs where the men can drink their 'pint' at the end of the work day or during a break.

No one has to walk around hungry in Belgium for lack of a convenient restaurant. There are innumerable food stands that sell French fries with mussels, sausages, mayonnaise, pickles and relish.

Ardennes, the tourist sees in almost every butcher's window cured hams packed in red-and-white checkered sacks waiting to be taken home as souvenirs. Belgians know and appreciate fine wines, but the national drink of Belgium is indisputably beer. Belgians are among the greatest beer drinkers in the world: the average consumption for each man, woman and child is 37 gallons a year. Each small village had its own brewery, and in the country you could hear the echoing sound of heavy brewer's horses drawing beer carts over stone roads, delivering beer to farms and small country cafés. In addition to the familiar lager beer, there is another type of beer brewed in Belgium. This is produced in the medieval manner, not with pure laboratory cultivated yeast, but with natural, local yeast which causes the beer to ferment slowly and acquire a distinctive flavor which differs sharply from place to place, and even from brewery to brewery. Brussels is especially proud of its own traditional beer, called 'geuze lambiek,' in which sour cherries are allowed to ferment. This gives the beer a quite unique sour flavor. This Brussels beer is brewed in many small breweries and delivered to a number of tiny cafés which are permanent customers. Beer connoisseurs maintain that the beer has a different taste in each part of Brussels and claim that

Belgium is a land rich in folklore, feasts, carnivals and fairs. On these occasions, the people dress in colorful medieval costumes and the day always begins with a procession through the streets of the town, accompanied by music and colorful banners. The flag is raised over the town hall, and the day invariably ends in one of the hundreds of cafés, where the people literally sing until their throats are dry and then drink gallons of beer and eat mussels, shrimp, sausages and the other specialities of the region.

they can distinguish at least 40 different types. The people of Brussels prefer to drink their beer in cafés (called staminées) with small dried fish or cottage cheese and large radishes. Patersbier (literally, 'fathers' beer) is equally famous. Its name comes from the fact that it is brewed by the monks of various abbeys. Each monastic order has its own method of brewing, following medieval traditions and using natural local yeasts. Famous examples of these beers come from the Trappist monks (considered by many the 'champagne' of beer) and from the Norbertine monks. Some of the larger abbeys have a beer cafe as well as a brewery where the fathers served their own beer, preferably in elegant, stemmed goblets, with cloister-baked bread, ham from their own smokehouses and cheese from their own dairy. These abbeys are the well-loved destination of many weekend trips for the whole family, for Belgian children are just as fond of beer as their parents.

Belgium also produces many kinds of cheese, but none quite as famous as the Dutch cheeses, except for the Hervée made at the foot of the Ardennes near the city of Liège. It is a cheese with a very penetrating aroma, but a gourmet delicacy that goes extraordinarily well with patersbier.

Snacks and entrees

Both in the Netherlands and Belgium, meals often begin with an appetizing fish course. Both these countries lie on the sea and both have well-stocked streams, ponds and canals.

During the years before the Second World War, a taste for lobster cocktail spread to Holland from the United States. But lobster is very expensive in the Netherlands, and the Dutch have turned to the smaller, but equally delectable shrimp that can be caught along the sandy coasts.

Shrimp cocktail has thus become a typical Dutch hors d'oeuvres, served in all Dutch restaurants and prepared at home on festive occasions.

Dutch housewives make fresh and attractive, soft-pink salads from the famous 'maatjes' herrings. The salty flavor of the herring blends to perfection with the sweet flavor of red beets.

The pride of any housewife from Flanders (the northwestern part of Belgium) is 'eel in green.' This is tender eel from the rivers of the lush Flemish landscape, served in a slightly sour, light-green sauce of eggs and fresh herbs. As soon as 'eel in green' appears (it is a typical summer dish), the restaurants hang up special red and black printed notices over their windows.

Garnalencocktail

Shrimp cocktail

6 servings

- 2 cups mayonnaise
- 1 tablespoon lemon juice
- 1 tablespoon dry white wine or sherry
  Dash of Worcestershire sauce
- 1 hard boiled egg, finely chopped
- 2 tablespoons grated apple
- 2 tablespoons finely chopped celery
- ¼ teaspoon salt
  Freshly ground black pepper
- 2 cups cooked small shrimp
- 2 teaspoons capers
- 2 tablespoons finely chopped chives
- 1 lemon, thinly sliced

Mix mayonnaise with the lemon juice, white wine and Worcestershire sauce. Stir in egg, apple and celery. Season with salt and pepper. Gently fold the shrimp into the mixture, reserving a few for garnish. Serve the cocktail in glass dishes and garnish with the remaining shrimp, capers, chives and lemon slices.

Garnalen-rijstsalade

Shrimp and rice salad

4 servings

- ½ pound small shrimp, cooked and shelled
- 2½ cups cooked rice
- 1 tablespoon finely chopped parsley
- 2 large tomatoes, peeled, seeded and cubed
- 4 tablespoons oil
- 2 tablespoons lemon juice
- 1 teaspoon prepared (Dijon type) mustard
- 2 teaspoons finely chopped onion
- ½ teaspoon salt
  Freshly ground black pepper
- 2 hard boiled eggs, shelled
- ½ cucumber, thinly sliced

Combine the shrimp, rice, parsley and tomatoes in a large bowl. Prepare a salad dressing with the oil, lemon juice, mustard, onion, salt and pepper. Pour the dressing over the shrimp mixture and toss gently. Let the salad rest 15 minutes. Mix well and transfer to a glass bowl or attractive serving dish. Cut the eggs into wedges and garnish the salad with the eggs and cucumber slices.

Tomates farcies aux crevettes

Stuffed tomatoes

4 servings

- 8 small tomatoes
- 1 cup cooked shrimp
- 1 small onion or scallion, finely chopped
- 2 tablespoons mayonnaise
- 1 tablespoon tomato catsup
- ¼ teaspoon salt
  Freshly ground black pepper
  Dash of Worcestershire sauce
- 8 sprigs parsley

Cut off the tops of the tomatoes and spoon out the pulp. Place upside down on paper towels to drain. Mix shrimp with the onion, mayonnaise and catsup. Season with salt, pepper and Worcestershire sauce. Stuff tomatoes with this mixture and decorate with a sprig of parsley.

Paling in het groen

Eel in green sauce

4 servings

*1½ to 2 pounds eels, skinned
  and cleaned
3 tablespoons butter
2 shallots or scallions,
  finely chopped
½ teaspoon sage
¼ teaspoon thyme
¼ teaspoon tarragon
2 tablespoons finely chopped
  parsley
½ teaspoon salt
  Freshly ground black pepper
¾ cup dry white wine
½ cup water
3 egg yolks, lightly beaten
  Juice of ½ lemon*

Cut the eels into 2 inch lengths.
Heat the butter in a skillet and
sauté them over moderately
high heat until lightly browned.
Add shallots, sage, thyme,
tarragon, parsley, salt, pepper,
white wine and just enough
water to barely cover the eels.
Bring to a simmer, cover the pan
and cook slowly for 6 to 8
minutes or until the eels are just
tender. Remove the eels to a
glass serving dish. Stir a little
of the hot liquid into the egg
yolks. Pour the egg yolk mixture
and the lemon juice into the
liquid in the skillet and stir with
a wire whisk over very low heat
until slightly thickened. Do not
allow the mixture to boil. Pour
the sauce over the eels and place
in the refrigerator. Serve cold.
Note: If eels are not available
in your area and you would like
to serve an approximation of
this dish, try it with lobster tails
or shrimp.

Salade van bloemkool en garnalen

Cauliflower and shrimp salad

4 servings

*1 small cauliflower
½ cup mayonnaise
1 teaspoon mustard
1 tablespoon finely chopped
  parsley
1 tablespoon tomato puree
1 tablespoon finely chopped
  chives
¼ teaspoon salt
  Freshly ground black pepper
½ pound small shrimp, cooked
  and shelled*

Divide the cauliflower into
flowerets and cook until tender
in boiling salted water. Cool the
cauliflower. Combine the
mayonnaise with the mustard,
parsley, tomato purée, chives,
salt and pepper. Combine the
cauliflower and the shrimp and
toss with the mayonnaise. Let
the salad rest in a cool place for
30 minutes before serving.

Rolmops

Marinated herring

6 servings

*6 fresh herrings, filleted or 6
  herrings in brine
12 gherkins
1 lemon, thinly sliced
1 medium sized onion, cut
  into rings
3 bay leaves
1¾ cups vinegar
¼ cup water
1 tablespoon salt (omit salt
  if using herring in brine)*

If using whole herring in brine,
soak in cold water for 24 hours.
Remove the heads and tails and
fillet the herring. Roll each fillet
around 1 gherkin. Place the rolls
in a clean glass jar or crock.
Arrange the lemon slices, onion
rings and bay leaves between the
rolls. Combine the vinegar,
water and salt in a saucepan,
and bring to the boiling point.
Remove from the heat and cool.
Pour the cooled mixture over
the herring rolls and cover the
jar. Let stand in the refrigerator
1 week before serving. The
rollmops will keep 3 to 4 weeks
in the refrigerator.

Haringsla

Herring salad

4 servings

> 2 salted herrings, filleted
> 3 medium sized cooked, cold potatoes, chopped
> 1 small cooked beet, peeled and chopped
> 2 cooking apples, peeled, cored and chopped
> 1 small onion, finely chopped
> 4 gherkins, finely chopped
> 2 hard boiled eggs
> 3 tablespoons salad oil
> 2 tablespoons vinegar
> ¼ teaspoon salt
>   Freshly ground black pepper
>   Mayonnaise
>   Lettuce leaves

Cut the herring fillets into small pieces. Reserve a few pieces for garnish. In a bowl which has been rinsed with cold water, combine herring, potatoes, beet, apples, onion, gherkins and one chopped hard boiled egg. Mix ingredients well and add salad oil, vinegar, salt and pepper. Press together firmly and unmold on a flat dish. Cover with a thin layer of mayonnaise and garnish with remaining pieces of herring, egg slices and lettuce leaves.

Huzarensla

The name for 'hussar's salad' (a Dutch rendition of what we know as Russian salad) originated in the small garrison towns where the hussars (mounted soldiers) were stationed. Given the quality of the food in the barracks, the average hussar was naturally anxious to get one of the kitchen maids as a girlfriend – preferably one that served a rich family. After the family's dinner, the hussar stole over to his girlfriend's kitchen to charm her into making him a salad out of leftovers.

Hussar's salad

4 servings

1½	cups chopped cold, cooked meat (veal or pork)
2	green apples, peeled, cored and chopped
1	small beet, cooked and chopped
2	hard boiled eggs
3	gherkins
1	small onion or scallion, finely chopped
8	small new potatoes, cooked, cooled and chopped
3	tablespoons oil
3	tablespoons vinegar
½	teaspoon salt
	Freshly ground black pepper
	Lettuce leaves
	Mayonnaise
1	tomato, peeled and thinly sliced

In a bowl, combine the meat, apples, beet, 1 egg, finely chopped, 2 chopped gherkins, onion and potatoes. Mix together the oil, vinegar, salt and pepper and pour over the salad. Toss to coat the meat and vegetables thoroughly. Place several lettuce leaves on a flat serving dish. Arrange the salad in a boat shape on the lettuce. Cover the "boat" with a very thin layer of mayonnaise. Decorate with thin slices of egg, gherkin and tomato.

Nierbroodjes

Kidney savories

4 servings

> 1 veal kidney (½ pound),
>   soaked in cold water for
>   1 hour
> 3 tablespoons butter
> 1 onion, finely chopped
> 6 tablespoons flour
> 1 cup beef broth
> 1 tablespoon tomato purée
> ½ teaspoon salt
>   Freshly ground black pepper
> 2 teaspoons Worcestershire
>   sauce
> 2 tablespoons Madeira or
>   sherry
> 4 slices white bread, crusts
>   removed
> 2 egg whites, lightly beaten
> 1 cup fine dry breadcrumbs
>   Oil for deep frying

Cut the kidney into thin slices.
Heat the butter and sauté the
kidney with the onion for
5 minutes. Stir in the flour, and
add the beef broth and tomato
purée, stirring constantly. Cook
for 3 minutes and season with
salt, pepper, Worcestershire
sauce and Madeira. Allow to
cool on a flat surface until set.
Cut the bread into squares
about 2½ inches × 2½ inches.
Cover the squares of bread
with a thick layer of the cold
kidney ragout. Coat with
breadcrumbs, dip in beaten egg
whites and again in breadcrumbs.
Heat oil for deep frying and
deep fry a few at a time, for
3 to 5 minutes. Drain on paper
towels. Serve piping hot.

Kamper steur

Eggs with mustard sauce

4 servings

> 4 hard boiled eggs
> 2 tablespoons butter
> 3 tablespoons flour
> 1¼ cups beef broth
> 1 tablespoon prepared
>   mustard
> 1 tablespoon chopped parsley

Halve the eggs lengthwise and
arrange on a warm serving dish.
Heat the butter, stir in the flour
and cook 2 minutes. Gradually
add the broth, stirring
constantly. Beat in the mustard.
Pour the sauce over the egg
halves and garnish with parsley.
Serve hot toasted bread and
butter separately.

Sneetje roerei
met champignons

Scrambled eggs with
mushrooms

4 servings

> 2 tablespoons butter
> 2 shallots or scallions, finely
>   chopped
> 1 cup thinly sliced mushrooms
> 6 eggs
> 6 tablespoons milk
> ¼ teaspoon salt
>   Freshly ground black pepper
>   Dash of nutmeg
> 4 slices toasted bread, crusts
>   removed

Heat the butter in a frying pan.
Add shallots and mushrooms
and sauté for 3 minutes. In the
meantime, beat the eggs with
the milk and add this mixture
to the pan, stirring constantly
until the eggs are set but still
creamy. Season with salt, pepper
and nutmeg and serve on hot
toasted bread.

Belgische kalfspaté

Belgian veal pâté

16 servings

- 2 pounds ground veal
- ½ pound ground calves' liver
- 1 small onion, finely chopped
- 1 egg, lightly beaten
- ½ cup sour cream
- 2 tablespoons finely chopped parsley
- 2 teaspoons salt
  Freshly ground black pepper
  Dash of nutmeg
- 1 tablespoon Madeira or sherry
- ½ pound thinly sliced bacon

Mix together all the ingredients except the bacon and beat until thoroughly combined. Line a pâté mold with bacon strips and pack the veal mixture into the mold. Cover with the remaining bacon. Cover the mold with aluminum foil, then a lid. Place the pâté mold in a larger pan and add boiling water to come halfway up the sides of the mold. Bake in a preheated 350° oven for 1 hour. When the pâté is done, remove the lid and place a brick or other heavy weight on the pâté. Refrigerate overnight. Unmold the pâté and remove the bacon. Serve, sliced very thinly, and arrange slices on a bed of lettuce leaves.

Kaasstokjes

Cheese sticks

50 to 60 sticks

- 1½ cups grated Gouda cheese
- 1¾ sticks butter, softened
- 1 egg yolk
- ½ teaspoon salt
- 1½ teaspoons Worcestershire sauce
- 3 cups flour

Combine ¾ cup cheese and all the remaining ingredients and mix until well blended. Wrap the dough in wax paper and refrigerate for 2 hours. Roll the dough out to a ¼ inch thickness and cut into strips 3 inches long and ¼ inch wide. Coat the sticks with the remaining grated cheese and arrange them on a buttered baking sheet. Bake in a preheated 400° oven for 15 minutes.

Kaastruffels

Cheese truffles

- 1¼ cups butter, softened
- 1 cup grated Gouda or Edam cheese
- ½ teaspoon salt
  Freshly ground black pepper
  Pinch of cayenne pepper
- ½ teaspoon Worcestershire sauce
- 6 slices stale dark pumpernickel bread, finely crumbled

Blend together the butter, cheese, salt, pepper, cayenne pepper and Worcestershire sauce until a smooth paste is formed. Shape into balls 1 inch in diameter and roll the balls in the bread crumbs. Refrigerate for 1 hour or until firm. Serve as a snack with cheese balls and cheese zebras.

Kaaszebra's

Cheese zebras

4 servings

- 6 tablespoons butter
- 4 egg yolks from hard boiled eggs, sieved
- ¼ teaspoon salt
  Freshly ground black pepper
  Few drops Worcestershire sauce
- 2 tablespoons grated Parmesan or Gouda cheese
- 4 thin slices dark pumpernickel bread

Beat the butter until soft. Blend in the egg yolks, salt, pepper, Worcestershire sauce and cheese until the mixture is smooth. Cover a slice of pumpernickel bread with a layer of this paste, exactly as thick as the slice of pumpernickel bread. Alternate layers of cheese paste with pumpernickel bread. Wrap in aluminum foil and chill in the refrigerator for at least 2½ hours. Cut with a sharp knife into thin slices. Arrange the "zebra's" on a platter garnished with lettuce leaves.

A typical Dutch cocktail platter with cheese truffles (recipe page 19, 3rd column), cheese zebras (recipe page 19, 4th column) and cheese balls.

Kaasbolletjes

Cheese balls

1¾ cups flour
1½ cups grated Gouda or
    Edam cheese
  1 teaspoon salt
    Freshly ground black pepper
 10 tablespoons butter
  3 egg yolks

Place the flour, cheese, salt and pepper in a bowl. Cut the butter into the flour mixture with a pastry blender or 2 knives until the mixture resembles coarse meal. Add the egg yolks and mix in with a fork. The mixture will be very crumbly. Gather the mixture together with your hands. Transfer to a very lightly floured board and knead until the dough is elastic. (It will spring back slightly on itself.) Shape the dough into a ball, wrap in waxed paper and refrigerate for 2 hours. Roll little bits of dough between the palms of your hands to shape ½ inch balls. Place the balls on a lightly buttered cookie sheet and bake in a preheated 375° oven for 15 to 20 minutes or until golden brown.

Meat croquettes (recipe page 22, 1st column)

Bitterballen

Traditionally in Holland, when the hour between five and six arrives and the day's work is over, it is time for an apéritif, a glass of Dutch gin or 'genever', called a 'borrel.'
Once gentlemen drank this cocktail in their clubs and workingmen drank theirs in bars or cafés. But most clubs have disappeared today, and it is increasingly fashionable to drink genever at home.
A snack must always accompany a 'borrel,' and alongside the good glass of genever there must be a square of good Dutch cheese with a dash of mustard. To make this a really festive occasion with friends, hot and spicy meat balls ('bitterballen') are served. These are crispy, golden-brown balls made with chopped meat, dipped in mustard and eaten with cocktail picks. Bitterballen are served so hot that foreign guests are warned not to pop them right into their mouths.

Savory balls

35 to 40 balls

  3 tablespoons butter
  5 tablespoons flour
  1 cup chicken broth
½ pound cold cooked veal, shredded
  1 tablespoon finely chopped parsley
½ teaspoon salt
     Freshly ground black pepper
  1 teaspoon Worcestershire sauce
     Oil for deep frying
  2 egg whites, beaten until foamy
½ cup fine dry breadcrumbs
     Prepared (Dijon type) mustard

Heat the butter in a saucepan, add the flour and cook, stirring, for 2 minutes. Gradually add the broth, stirring constantly until a thick paste is formed. Add the veal, parsley, salt, pepper and Worcestershire sauce and combine thoroughly. Spread the mixture on a plate and refrigerate for 2 hours. Heat the oil for deep frying. Form the veal mixture into 1 inch balls. Dip the balls in the egg white, then roll in the breadcrumbs. Deep fry a few balls at a time for 2 minutes or until golden. Drain on paper towels. Serve piping hot on wooden cocktail picks and pass mustard for dipping.
Note: This is a well known appetizer in Holland and the bitterballs are usually served with a glass of ice cold "genever" (Dutch gin).

Vleeskroketten

Meat croquettes

8 servings

    3 tablespoons butter
    5 tablespoons flour
    1 cup beef broth
    ½ pound cold, cooked lean veal,
      shredded
    ¼ teaspoon salt
      Freshly ground black pepper
      Dash of nutmeg
    ¼ teaspoon Worcestershire
      sauce
    1 cup fine dry bread crumbs
    2 egg whites
      Oil for deep frying
      Parsley sprigs for garnish

Heat butter, stir in flour and cook 2 minutes. Gradually add the beef broth, stirring constantly until a smooth paste is formed. Add the veal, salt, pepper, nutmeg and Worcestershire sauce. Spread out on a flat surface and refrigerate until firm. When set, cut into 8 equal parts and form cylinders 3″ long and 1″ in diameter. Roll each in bread crumbs, then in beaten egg whites, then again in bread crumbs. See that each croquette is completely coated with bread crumbs. Deep fry in hot oil a few at a time for 3 to 5 minutes. Drain and serve piping hot, garnished with parsley.

Croquettes de moules

Mussel croquettes

8 croquettes

    3 pounds fresh mussels or 1
      (8 ounce) can mussels
    4 tablespoons butter
    6 tablespoons flour
    ¾ cup milk
    ½ cup thinly sliced mushrooms
    1 cup fine dry breadcrumbs
    2 egg whites, lightly beaten
      Oil for deep frying
      Few sprigs parsley

Wash and scrub fresh mussels. Cook them, covered, in 1½ to 2 cups boiling water for 7 to 10 minutes or until the shells open. Remove mussels from the shells and reserve 1 cup cooking liquid. If canned mussels are used, reserve the liquid from the can and add enough water to make 1 cup. In a saucepan, heat the butter, stir in the flour and cook 2 minutes. Add the reserved liquid and the milk gradually, beating constantly with a wire whisk until the sauce is smooth and very thick. Add the mussels and mushrooms and cook 5 minutes. Place the mixture in a shallow flat dish and refrigerate for 2 hours or until the mixture is quite firm. Divide into 8 equal parts and form each into a cylinder 3 inches long and 1 inch in diameter. Roll each cylinder in breadcrumbs, dip in the egg white and roll again in breadcrumbs. Heat the oil for deep frying and fry the croquettes, a few at a time, for 3 to 5 minutes. Drain on paper towels. Serve piping hot garnished with parsley sprigs.

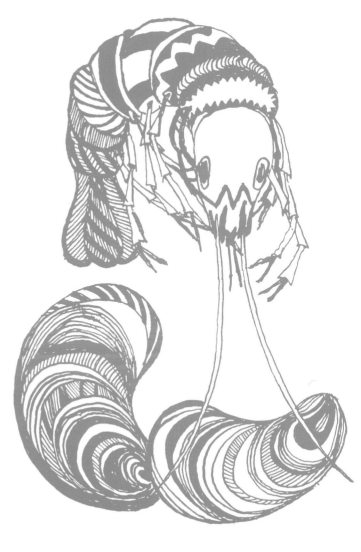

Garnalenkroketten

Shrimp croquettes

4 servings

2 tablespoons butter
4 tablespoons flour
1 cup milk
1 cup cooked small shrimp, shelled
½ teaspoon salt
Freshly ground black pepper
Juice of ½ lemon
1 teaspoon Worcestershire sauce
1 cup fine dry breadcrumbs
2 egg whites, lightly beaten
Oil for deep frying
Few sprigs parsley

Heat the butter, stir in flour and add milk gradually, stirring until a thick sauce is formed. Add shrimp. Season with salt, pepper, lemon juice and Worcestershire sauce. Transfer mixture to a shallow flat dish and refrigerate until quite firm. Form 4 cylinders, about 3″ long and 1″ in diameter. Roll each cylinder in breadcrumbs, then in the egg whites and again in the breadcrumbs. Heat oil for deep frying and fry the croquettes in hot oil for 3 to 5 minutes. Drain on paper towels. Serve piping hot, garnished with parsley.

Brusselse sardinebroodjes

Brussels sardine sandwiches

6 servings

12 canned sardines
1 hard boiled egg, finely chopped
2 teaspoons prepared (Dijon type) mustard
3 teaspoons lemon juice
1 teaspoon grated onion
2 teaspoons finely chopped parsley
6 thin slices white bread, crusts removed
3 tablespoons butter
1 dill pickle sliced or
½ lemon sliced

Finely flake the sardines with a fork and combine with the egg, mustard, lemon juice, onion, parsley and 3 teaspoons oil from the sardine can. Cut the pieces of bread in half diagonally and sauté in the butter until golden brown on both sides. Spread the sardine mixture on the slices of bread while they are still warm and garnish with halved, very thinly sliced pickle or lemon.

Saucijzebroodjes

Sausage rolls

10 servings

1 pound lean ground pork
1 teaspoon salt
Freshly ground black pepper
Dash of nutmeg

For the dough:
1 package dry yeast
1¼ cups lukewarm water
4 cups flour
1½ teaspoons salt
4 tablespoons melted butter

Season the ground pork with salt, pepper and nutmeg and set aside. Sprinkle the yeast over the lukewarm water and stir to dissolve. Place the flour and salt in a bowl and make a well in the center. Pour the butter and dissolved yeast into the well and gather the dough into a ball. Knead the dough on a floured board for 8 to 10 minutes or until the dough is smooth and elastic. Shape the dough into a ball and place in an oiled bowl. Cover and let rise 2 hours or until doubled in bulk. Knead the dough again and divide into 10 pieces. Roll each piece into a square, 6 inches by 6 inches. Make 10 rolls of the ground pork and place one on each square of dough. Fold the dough over the pork rolls. Place the rolls on a buttered baking sheet and let rise in a warm place for another 3 hours or until doubled in bulk. Place the baking sheet in a preheated, 350° oven and bake for 45 minutes.

Soups

Dutch pea soup

Chicken soup is a traditional Sunday dish both in Holland and in Belgium.

Hollandse erwtensoep

The national soup of the Netherlands is pea soup. There are as many varieties as there are cooks in Holland. Pea soup is prepared in a different way in each family and every housewife has her own secret recipe. Inevitably, Dutch men always boast about the pea soup that their wives and mothers make. According to the traditional standard, pea soup, to be any good, must be so thick that a spoon will stand up in it. This is the way soup used to be served in the Dutch navy and so this thick soup has been named 'naval pea soup.'

As soon as the first cold days come in October and November, cafés and restaurants hang a sign over their windows notifying customers that the soup is ready. And the same soup is served at all train stations in winter. When canals and lakes are frozen over and people make long trips on ice skates over the weekend, it is a 'must' to stop at one of the small inns along the way to eat pea soup with bacon and sausage.

Dutch pea soup

6 to 8 servings (main course)

1½ cups green split peas
  3 quarts water
  2 pigs' feet (opt.)
1½ teaspoons salt
  3 leeks, thinly sliced or
  2 medium sized yellow onions, sliced
  1 stalk celery, chopped
  3 medium sized potatoes, peeled and cubed
    Leafy tops from 1 bunch of celery
 ½ pound piece fat ham or
  1 large smoked sausage or
 ½ pound frankfurters, sliced
    Slices of pumpernickel bread

Soak the peas in water to cover overnight. Drain the peas and place them in a large pan with the water, pigs' feet and salt. Bring to a boil, lower the heat and simmer slowly for 3 hours. Add leeks, celery, potatoes and celery tops and simmer another 30 minutes, stirring occasionally. Add sausage or frankfurters and simmer 10 minutes more. Discard the pigs' feet. Remove ham, sausage or frankfurters. Slice sausage and serve on buttered pumpernickel bread accompanied by bowls of the hot soup.

Kippesoep met balletjes

Chicken soup with meat balls

4 servings

      2 *pounds stewing chicken*
 $3\frac{1}{2}$ *cups water*
 $2\frac{1}{2}$ *teaspoons salt*
         Freshly ground black pepper
 $\frac{1}{4}$ *teaspoon basil*
      1 *bay leaf*
 $\frac{1}{4}$ *teaspoon mace*
      1 *small clove garlic,*
         crushed
 $\frac{1}{2}$ *pound small white onions*
      5 *small carrots, sliced*
      1 *tablespoon finely chopped*
         combined parsley and
         celery leaves

Place the chicken in the water in a large saucepan. Add the salt, pepper, basil, bay leaf, mace and garlic. Bring to a boil, lower the heat and simmer slowly for $1\frac{1}{2}$ hours or until the chicken is just tender. Remove chicken from the pan. Strain the broth and carefully skim the fat from the surface of the soup. Bring the soup to a boil and add the onions, carrots, parsley and celery and simmer gently for 10 minutes.

For the meat balls:
      1 *cup finely minced pork*
      1 *egg*
      1 *slice crumbled white bread,*
         crusts removed
 $2\frac{1}{2}$ *tablespoons flour*
 $\frac{1}{2}$ *teaspoon salt*
         Freshly ground black pepper

Mix pork with egg, bread, flour, salt and pepper. Form into small meat balls, about $\frac{3}{4}$ inch in diameter. Add the meat balls

to the soup and simmer for a further 35 minutes. Meanwhile, skin and bone the chicken. Cut the meat into small pieces and measure $\frac{1}{2}$ cup. Garnish the soup with the chicken and serve. Save the remaining chicken for use in salads or sandwiches.

Zomer groentesoep

Vegetable summer soup

6 servings

- 3 tablespoons butter
- 6 small carrots, peeled and sliced
- 6 cauliflower flowerets
- 1 leek, chopped
- ½ cup young green peas
- 6 cups beef broth, simmering
- 3 tablespoons uncooked rice
- ½ teaspoon salt
  Freshly ground black pepper
- 1 tablespoon finely chopped mixed garden herbs (chervil, chives, parsley, celery tops)
- 2 tomatoes, peeled and cut in wedges
- 1½ tablespoons cornstarch dissolved in 3 tablespoons water

For the meatballs:
- ½ cup ground veal
- ¼ teaspoon salt
  Freshly ground black pepper
  Dash of nutmeg
  Flour

Heat the butter in a large saucepan. Add the carrots, cauliflower, leek and peas and cook slowly for 10 minutes. Add the broth, rice, salt and pepper and bring to a boil. Reduce the heat and simmer slowly 15 minutes. Meanwhile, combine the veal, salt, pepper and nutmeg and form into balls ½ inch in diameter. Roll the meatballs in flour. Add the meatballs to the soup and simmer 15 minutes more. Stir in the garden herbs, tomatoes and cornstarch mixture and simmer a few minutes until the soup has thickened slightly. Serve immediately.

Preisoep

Belgian leek soup

4 to 6 servings

- 3 tablespoons butter
- ½ pound leeks, sliced or
- 4 yellow onions, sliced
- 1 pound potatoes, peeled and cubed
- 6 cups beef broth
- 1 teaspoon salt
- ½ cup cream or milk
- 4–6 slices toasted French bread

Heat the butter in a large saucepan. Add the leeks and sauté 3 minutes. Then add the cubed potatoes, beef broth and salt. Bring to a boil and cook for 40 minutes, stirring occasionally. Before serving, stir in cream or milk. Place a slice of toasted bread in each soup bowl and pour the hot soup over the bread.

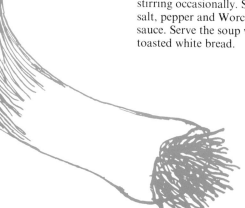

Bruine bonensoep

Brown bean soup

6 servings (main course)

- 1½ cups dried kidney beans
- 3 quarts water
- 1 bay leaf
- 2 cloves
- 3 medium sized potatoes, peeled and cubed
- 3 tablespoons butter
- 1 onion, chopped
- ½ tablespoon curry powder
- 1 teaspoon salt
  Freshly ground black pepper
  Dash of Worcestershire sauce

Soak the beans in the water overnight. Bring to a boil, add the bay leaf and cloves and cook for 2 hours. Add potatoes and cook for another 30 minutes. In the meantime, heat the butter in a frying pan and sauté the chopped onion and curry powder until light brown. Remove bay leaf and cloves from the soup. Strain the broth and purée beans and potatoes in the blender. Add the purée to the broth. Add sautéed onion and cook for another 20 minutes, stirring occasionally. Season with salt, pepper and Worcestershire sauce. Serve the soup with toasted white bread.

Soupe mosane

Soup from the Meuse

4 to 6 servings

   3 tablespoons butter
   1 head Boston lettuce,
      shredded
   4 scallions, sliced
   1 stalk celery, chopped
   6 cups water
   ½ pound fresh green peas
   ½ pound cooked ham, in 1 piece
   1 teaspoon thyme
   1 bay leaf
   ¼–½ teaspoons salt (depending
      on saltiness of ham)
      Freshly ground black pepper
   ½ cup cream or milk
   2 tablespoons finely chopped
      chervil or parsley

Heat the butter in a large
saucepan and sauté the lettuce,
scallions and celery slowly for
10 minutes. Add water, peas,
ham, thyme, bay leaf, salt and
pepper. Bring to a boil, lower
the heat and simmer slowly for
1 hour. Remove the ham and
cut into small pieces. Strain the
broth and purée the vegetables
in the blender. Return the ham
and puréed vegetables to the
broth. Add the cream and heat
the soup thoroughly but do not
boil. Serve in individual bowls
and garnish each serving with a
little chervil or parsley.

Humpkessoep

Vegetable soup

6 to 8 servings

   8 cups water
   1 pound green beans, cut into
      1 inch pieces
   1 pound smoked sausage or
      frankfurters
   4 medium sized onions,
      chopped
   4 medium sized potatoes,
      peeled and diced
   1 cup mixed soup vegetables
      (celery tops, leeks, carrots,
      etc.)
   1 teaspoon salt
      Freshly ground black pepper
   2 tomatoes, peeled and cut
      into wedges
   4 tablespoons finely chopped
      parsley

Bring the water to a boil in a
large saucepan. Add the green
beans, lower the heat and
simmer 10 minutes. Add all the
remaining ingredients except
the tomatoes and parsley and
simmer 30 minutes. Just before
serving, stir in the tomatoes
and parsley and simmer
2 minutes.

Soupe au lard

Bacon soup

6 servings

   ½ pound bacon, in 1 piece
   6 cups cold water
   12 peppercorns, crushed
   2 bay leaves
   1 teaspoon thyme
   3 large carrots, peeled and
      sliced
   2 small leeks, sliced
   3 stalks celery, sliced
   3 turnips, cubed
   ¼ small cabbage, shredded
      Salt, if necessary

Soak the bacon in cold water for
3 hours, changing the water
frequently. (This will reduce the
saltiness of the bacon.) Place
the 6 cups cold water in a heavy
pan and add the bacon,
peppercorns, bay leaves and
thyme. Bring to a boil, skim and
lower the heat. Cover the pan
and cook over the lowest
possible heat for 30 minutes.
Add the vegetables. Taste the
broth and add salt, if necessary.
This will depend on the saltiness
of your bacon. Continue to
simmer the soup, covered, for
1 hour. Remove the bacon
from the pan. Discard the fat,
cut the meat into small pieces
and return to the soup.
Refrigerate the soup and lift off
the fat when it has risen to the
top. When ready to serve,
reheat the soup briefly.

Niersoep

Kidney soup

4 servings

   1 veal kidney (about ½
      pound)
   4 cups beef broth
   ½ teaspoon salt
      Freshly ground black pepper
   3 tablespoons butter
   1 tablespoon finely chopped
      onion
   4 tablespoons flour
   1 cup cream
   1 cup thinly sliced
      mushrooms
   2 tablespoons Madeira or
      dry sherry

Soak kidney in cold water
2 hours, changing the water
twice. Drain and slice kidney
thinly. Add the slices to the
beef broth and season with
salt and pepper. Bring to a boil,
lower the heat and simmer
30 minutes. Strain the broth.
Heat the butter in a skillet and
sauté the onion until golden.
Add the flour and cook,
stirring for 1 to 2 minutes. Add
the cream and broth slowly,
stirring with a wire whisk to
form a smooth soup. Return
the kidneys to the soup, add the
mushrooms and cook 10
minutes more. Stir in the
Madeira or sherry just before
serving.

Mushroom soup

Chervil is the best loved soup in Belgium. You can buy bunches of fresh chervil all year round at any market and at any grocer's. The pleasant odor of chervil soup is familiar to anyone who has stayed in a Belgian boarding house.

Champignonsoep

Mushroom soup

6 servings

- 4 tablespoons butter
- 1 pound fresh mushrooms, thinly sliced
- 2 tablespoons flour
- 6 cups beef broth, simmering
- $\frac{1}{2}$ teaspoon salt
  Freshly ground black pepper
- 1 egg yolk combined with 2 tablespoons cream
  Juice of $\frac{1}{2}$ lemon
- 2 slices white bread, diced and toasted in the oven until brown

Heat the butter in a large saucepan and sauté the mushrooms over medium heat for 3 to 4 minutes. Stir in the flour and cook 2 minutes. Add the hot broth gradually, stirring constantly. Season with salt and pepper and simmer slowly 10 minutes. Just before serving, stir in the egg yolk mixed with cream and the lemon juice. Heat the soup, but do not allow it to boil. Top each serving with toasted croutons.

Kervelsoep

Chervil soup

4 to 6 servings

- 3 tablespoons butter
- 2 tablespoons flour
- 6 cups beef broth
- $\frac{1}{2}$ teaspoon salt
  Freshly ground black pepper
- 1 egg yolk
- $\frac{1}{4}$ cup cream
- 2 tablespoons finely chopped fresh chervil or parsley

In a saucepan, heat the butter, add flour and stir into a smooth paste. Add beef broth gradually, stirring constantly. Cook for 3 minutes. Season with salt and pepper. Combine egg yolk, cream and fresh chervil in a soup tureen and, stirring constantly, very carefully pour the hot soup over the mixture. Ladle the soup into individual bowls and serve at once.

The Belgians, like the French, prefer to use a somewhat old, toughened rooster for their Sunday soup because this gives body to the broth. They say the more adventures the rooster has had, the more it contributes to the soup. (recipe page 30, 4th column).

Soupe du Dimanche

Sunday soup

6 servings

      8 *cups water*
      1 *pound chicken, cut into pieces*
      1 *carrot, peeled*
    ½ *small onion, chopped*
      1 *sprig parsley*
    ½ *cup leafy celery tops*
      1 *clove garlic, crushed*
    ¼ *teaspoon thyme*
      1 *bay leaf*
    ½ *teaspoon salt*
      6 *peppercorns, crushed*
      1 *slice white bread, crusts removed*
      2 *tablespoons milk*
    ¼ *pound ground beef*
         Dash of nutmeg
    ¼ *teaspoon salt*
         Freshly ground black pepper
      3 *tablespoons flour*

Place the water, chicken, carrot, onion, parsley, celery, garlic, thyme, bay leaf, salt and peppercorns in a heavy pan and bring to a boil. Lower the heat, cover and simmer slowly 2 hours. Soak the bread in milk and blend with the ground beef, nutmeg, salt, pepper and flour. Knead into a stiff mixture and shape into small balls. Strain the the broth and return the broth to the pan. Cut the chicken meat into small pieces and slice the carrot. Simmer the meatballs in the broth for 30 minutes. Add chicken meat and carrot and cook 5 minutes more.

Vermicellisoep met balletjes

Vermicelli soup with meat balls

6 servings

For the meat balls:
- ¼ *cup ground veal*
- ¼ *cup ground pork*
- ¼ *teaspoon salt*
- *Freshly ground black pepper*
- *Dash of nutmeg*
- *Flour*

For the soup:
- 6 *cups beef broth*
- ⅔ *cup broken vermicelli*

Prepare meat balls by mixing ground veal, ground pork, salt, pepper and nutmeg. Form into small balls about ½ inch in diameter and coat the meatballs with flour. Bring the broth to a boil, add the broken vermicelli and the meat balls and simmer for about 15 minutes. Taste the broth for seasoning and add salt and pepper if necessary. Serve immediately.

Koninginnesoep

Queen's soup

4 servings

- 3 *tablespoons butter*
- 3 *tablespoons flour*
- 4 *cups chicken broth*
- ½ *cup finely chopped cooked chicken*
- ¼ *teaspoon salt*
- *Freshly ground black pepper*
- 1 *egg yolk combined with 4 tablespoons cream*

Heat the butter, add the flour and stir into a smooth paste. Gradually add the chicken broth, stirring constantly. Bring to a simmer, add the chicken meat, salt and pepper and cook for 3 minutes. Add the egg yolk mixture and stir with a wire whisk just until heated through. Do not allow the soup to boil after the egg yolk is added. Serve immediately.

Kruudmoes

Milk soup with barley

6 servings

- ¾ *cup barley, soaked overnight in water to cover*
- 2 *quarts buttermilk*
- ¼ *pound lean salt pork, diced*
- 4 *frankfurters, sliced*
- 1 *cup raisins*
- ¼ *teaspoon chervil*
- ¼ *teaspoon thyme*
- *Brown sugar or molasses*

Drain the barley and place in a heavy pan with the buttermilk and salt pork. Bring to a simmer, cover and cook slowly for 2 hours. Add frankfurters and raisins and simmer 15 minutes more. Stir in the chervil and thyme. Serve in individual bowls and pass a dish of brown sugar or molasses as a topping for the soup. This may be served hot or cold.

Aspergesoep

Asparagus soup

6 servings

- 1½ *pounds fresh asparagus*
- 3 *tablespoons butter*
- 4 *tablespoons flour*
- 6 *cups chicken broth, simmering*
- ½ *teaspoon salt*
- *Freshly ground black pepper*
- 1 *egg yolk, combined with 2 tablespoons milk*

Wash the asparagus. Cut off and discard any woody ends. Remove the tender asparagus tips and reserve. Cut the stalks into 1 inch pieces. In a large saucepan, heat the butter. Stir in the flour and cook 2 minutes. Add the hot broth gradually, stirring with a wire whisk until smooth. Add the asparagus stalks, salt and pepper and simmer slowly 20 to 25 minutes or until the asparagus is tender. Purée the soup in a blender and pass it through a sieve to remove the stringy part of the asparagus. Reheat the soup, add the asparagus tips and simmer slowly about 7 minutes. Stir in the egg yolk combined with the milk but do not allow the soup to boil. Serve immediately.

Potage aux carottes

Ossestaartsoep

Carrot soup

6 to 8 servings

- ¼ *pound lean bacon, cut in small pieces*
- 1 *medium sized onion, finely chopped*
- 6 *cups water*
- 1 *stalk celery, chopped*
- ½ *pound carrots, peeled and sliced*
- ½ *pound potatoes, peeled and cubed*
- ½ *teaspoon salt*
  Freshly ground black pepper
- 1 *teaspoon sugar*
- ¼ *teaspoon mace*
- ¼ *teaspoon thyme*
- 1 *bay leaf*
- ½ *cup cream or milk*
- 1 *tablespoon finely chopped chervil or parsley*
- 2 *slices white bread, crusts removed*
- 2 *tablespoons butter*

Fry the bacon until the fat is rendered. Remove the bacon and discard all but 1 tablespoon bacon fat. Add the onion and sauté 5 minutes. In a saucepan, bring the water to a boil. Add the bacon, onion, celery, carrots, potatoes, salt, pepper, sugar, mace, thyme and bay leaf. Simmer, covered, for 1 hour. Purée the soup in a blender and pour it through a sieve back into the saucepan. Add the cream and chervil and heat the soup but do not boil. Cut the slices of bread in quarters diagonally and sauté in the butter until golden brown on both sides. Float the bread triangles on individual servings of soup.

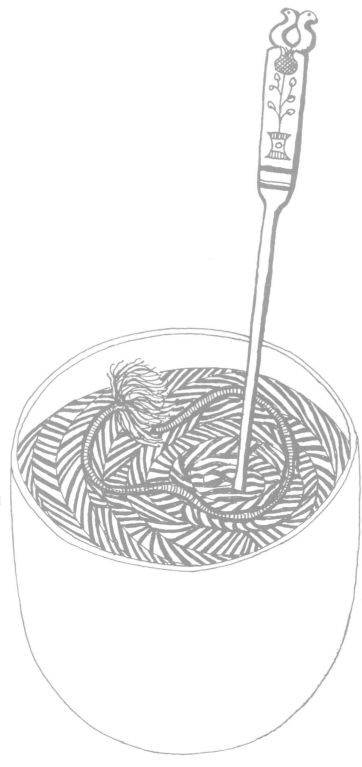

Oxtail soup

4 to 6 servings

- 1 *small piece salt pork or bacon*
- 1 *oxtail, cut into pieces at the joints*
- ½ *teaspoon salt*
  Freshly ground black pepper
- ½ *teaspoon thyme*
- 1 *bay leaf*
- 1 *sprig parsley*
- 8 *cups water*
- 4 *tablespoons barley or rice*
- 1 *medium sized carrot, sliced*
- 1 *leek, thinly sliced*
- 1 *onion, coarsely chopped*
- 1 *stalk celery, sliced*
- 1 *medium sized potato, peeled and cubed*
- ¼ *pound lean bacon, finely chopped*
- 1 *tablespoon Madeira or sherry*
- 2 *tablespoons finely chopped parsley*

Rub a large heavy pan with the salt pork. Place it in the pan with the oxtail, salt, pepper, thyme, bay leaf, parsley and water and bring to a boil. Lower the heat, partially cover and simmer slowly 4 hours. Strain the broth and remove the meat from the oxtail joints. Return the meat to the strained broth and add the barley or rice. Cover and cook over low heat 30 minutes. Add the carrot, leek, onion, celery, potato and bacon and simmer, covered, 30 minutes more. Taste for seasoning and add Madeira. Garnish each serving with parsley.

32

Shrimp from Ostende are famous. No fish soup in Ostende would ever be complete without them.

Oostendse vissoep

Fish soup from Ostende

6 servings

> Head and bones of 1 flounder or other salt-water fish
> 6 cups water
> Few sprigs parsley
> 1 small leek or onion, sliced
> 1 carrot, peeled and sliced
> 1 slice lemon
> 1 teaspoon salt
> 6 peppercorns, crushed
> 3 tablespoons flour
> 1 cup cooked, small shrimp, shelled
> 1 teaspoon tomato paste
> 2 teaspoons lemon juice
> ½ cup cream
> 1 tablespoon finely chopped parsley

Place the fish head and bones in a saucepan with the water. (Or use ½ bottled clam juice and ½ water if fish trimmings are not available.) Add the parsley, leek, carrot, lemon slice, salt (omit if clam juice is used) and peppercorns. Bring to a boil, lower the heat and simmer, covered, for 30 minutes. Strain the broth and discard fish trimmings and vegetables. Make a smooth mixture with the flour and ½ cup of the broth. Add the flour mixture to the broth gradually, stirring constantly with a wire whisk. Purée ½ cup of the shrimp in a blender with the tomato paste, lemon juice and a little of the cream. Add the shrimp purée and the cream to the soup and heat through but do not boil. Just before serving, stir in the remaining shrimp and the parsley.

Fish dishes

You have to use fresh water fish caught in the Flemish rivers and canals to make a real Flemish waterzooi (recipe page 34, 1st column).

Waterzooi van vis

Waterzooi of fish

6 servings

   *3 pounds fresh fish, filleted
      (pike, carp or bass)
      Leafy tops from 1 bunch
      celery
   2 tablespoons butter
   1 teaspoon salt
      Freshly ground black pepper
   3 egg yolks
   3 tablespoons cream
  12 slices rye bread
      Butter*

Cut the fish into 2 inch pieces. Place in a pan and just cover with water. Add celery leaves, butter, salt and pepper and cook over moderate heat about 8 to 10 minutes or until fish flakes easily. Do not overcook. Remove the fish and keep warm. Strain the broth, discard celery leaves and reduce fish broth to 2 cups. Beat the egg yolks with the cream. Stir 1 tablespoon of the broth into the egg yolks, then add this mixture to the hot broth, stirring constantly. Continue cooking until broth has thickened slightly but do not allow it to boil or the egg yolks will curdle. Pour the sauce over the fish and serve with buttered rye bread.

Gestoofde kabeljauwstaart

Stewed cod

4 servings

   *4 cod steaks
   1 teaspoon salt
   ½ cup water or fish broth
      Juice of ½ lemon
   2 tablespoons butter
   3 tablespoons fine dry bread
      crumbs
   ½ lemon, sliced
      Parsley sprigs*

Rub the cod with salt and let stand for 30 minutes. Place in an ovenproof dish with the water or fish broth. Sprinkle with lemon juice, dot with butter and sprinkle with bread crumbs. Cover with aluminum foil and bake in a preheated 300° oven for about 30 minutes. Garnish with lemon slices and parsley. Serve with small new potatoes or mashed potatoes and a salad.

Marine stokvis

Dried cod navy style

4 servings

   *1 pound salt cod
   4 cups water
   ½ teaspoon salt
   1 cup rice
   6 tablespoons butter
   3 tablespoons flour
   2 tablespoons prepared
      mustard
   2 onions, cut into rings
   4 eggs
   4 potatoes, cooked
   2 gherkins, chopped*

Soak the fish in water for 4 hours. Remove the bones, if any, and cut the meat into strips. Roll up and tie the strips. Bring the water to a boil, add the salt and cod and lower the heat. Simmer slowly for 1 hour. Keep the cod warm and reserve the cooking liquid. Cook the rice, following the directions on the package. Heat 3 tablespoons butter in a saucepan, stir in the flour and add 2 cups of the cooking liquid, stirring constantly until a smooth sauce is formed. Stir in mustard. In a frying pan heat the remaining 3 tablespoons butter and sauté the onion rings until golden brown. Serve cod, raw eggs, potatoes, rice, onion rings, gherkins and mustard sauce separately. In the Dutch navy, this dish is eaten as follows: In a deep plate combine raw egg with a potato. Mash well. Then mix the potato with the cod and rice. Spoon over the fried onion rings, gherkins and mustard sauce.

Vlaamse kabeljauw

Flemish cod

4 servings

   *4 cod fillets, ½ pound each
   ¼ cup butter
   1 onion, thinly sliced
   ½ cup warm water
   1 tablespoon lemon juice
   1 tablespoon freshly chopped
      parsley*

Butter an ovenproof dish with 2 tablespoons butter and place the cod fillets in the dish. Heat the remaining butter in a saucepan and sauté the onion over low heat until golden. Add the warm water and simmer 10 minutes. Spoon onions and liquid over the fish fillets. Cover the dish with aluminum foil and place in a preheated 300° oven for about 30 minutes. Uncover and sprinkle on the lemon juice and chopped parsley.

Makreel met prei

Vlaamse tarbot

Schelvis met mosterdsaus

Mackerel with leeks

4 servings

- 3 *leeks, white part only, thinly sliced or 3 white onions*
- 4 *tablespoons butter*
- ½ *cup fish broth*
- ¼ *teaspoon salt*
  Dash of nutmeg
- 2 *(1 pound) mackerel*
- ¼ *teaspoon powdered saffron*

Cook the leeks in boiling, salted water for 5 minutes and drain. In a small, heavy saucepan, melt 2 tablespoons butter. Add the leeks and sauté over low heat for several minutes without browning. Add the broth, salt and nutmeg. Place the mackerel in a buttered oven-proof dish and sprinkle with saffron. Spoon the leek mixture over the fish and dot with the remaining butter. Bake in a preheated 400° oven for 15 minutes.

Flemish turbot

4 servings

- 1½ *pounds turbot*
- 4 *cups water*
- 1 *teaspoon salt*
- 8 *peppercorns, crushed*
- ¼ *teaspoon thyme*
- 1 *bay leaf*
- 1 *tablespoon vinegar*
  Freshly chopped parsley
- ½ *cup butter, melted*
- 2 *teaspoons lemon juice*
- 2 *pounds new potatoes, cooked*

Cut the turbot into serving pieces. In a heavy saucepan, place the water, salt, peppercorns, thyme, bay leaf and vinegar and bring to a boil. Add the turbot, reduce the heat to a slow simmer and poach the fish for 15 to 20 minutes or until it flakes easily. Do not overcook. Drain the fish, place on a serving platter and surround with a ring of parsley. Add the lemon juice to the butter and pour over the potatoes. Serve the buttered potatoes with the turbot.

Haddock with mustard sauce

4 servings

- 2 *pounds haddock, filleted*
- 1 *teaspoon salt*
  Juice of 1 lemon
- 6 *cups water*
- 1 *tablespoon vinegar*
- 1 *onion, sliced*
- 1 *carrot*
  Few sprigs parsley
- ½ *teaspoon thyme*
- 8 *peppercorns, crushed*
- 1 *bay leaf*
- 2 *tablespoons finely chopped parsley*
- 1 *lemon, thinly sliced*
- 1 *recipe mustard sauce or curry sauce*

Rub the haddock fillets on both sides with salt and lemon juice. Place the water, vinegar, onion, carrot, parsley, thyme, peppercorns and bay leaf in a large saucepan and simmer 30 minutes. Add the fish and poach over low heat for 6 to 8 minutes. Do not overcook. Remove the fish and keep warm. (Strain the broth and use broth for the sauce.) To serve, place the fish on a heated platter and garnish with parsley and slices of lemon. Pass a mustard or a curry sauce separately.

Mustard sauce

- 3 *tablespoons butter*
- 3 *tablespoons flour*
- 2 *cups fish broth (from previous haddock recipe)*
- ¼ *teaspoon salt*
  Freshly ground black pepper
- ½ *cup white wine*
- 2 *tablespoons prepared (Dijon type) mustard*
- 3 *tablespoons heavy cream*

Heat the butter in a saucepan, add the flour and cook stirring for 2 minutes. Gradually add the fish broth, stirring constantly. Season with salt and pepper. Simmer for 15 minutes over moderate heat, stirring occasionally. Stir in the wine. Allow to boil for 3 minutes. Remove from the heat and stir in the mustard and cream. Served with poached haddock.

Curry sauce

- 3 *tablespoons butter*
- 1 *medium sized onion, finely chopped*
- 3 *tablespoons flour*
- 1 *tablespoon curry powder*
- 2 *cups fish broth (from previous haddock recipe)*
- ½ *teaspoon salt*
  Freshly ground black pepper
- 2 *tablespoons white wine*
- 3 *tablespoons heavy cream*

Heat the butter in a saucepan, add the onion and sauté for 3 minutes. Add the flour and curry powder and cook, stirring, for 2 minutes. Add the fish broth gradually, stirring constantly. Season to taste with salt and pepper. Simmer for 15 minutes over moderate heat, stirring occasionally. Stir in wine. Allow to simmer for 3 minutes. Remove from heat and stir in cream. Serve with poached haddock.

Haddock with mustard sauce (recipe page 35, 3rd column).

Paling op zijn Volendams

Stewed eel Volendam style

4 servings

    2 pounds eels, skinned and
      cleaned
    1 teaspoon salt
      Freshly ground black pepper
    ¼ teaspoon thyme
    ½ cup dry white wine
      Juice of ½ lemon
    2 bay leaves
    1 medium sized onion,
      thinly sliced
    ¼ cup fine dry breadcrumbs
    4 tablespoons butter
    1 cup chopped mixed dried
      fruits
    1 teaspoon cinnamon
      Mashed potatoes

Cut the eels into 2 inch pieces, sprinkle with the salt and let stand 5 minutes. Stand the pieces of eel upright in a casserole just large enough to hold them. Sprinkle with pepper and thyme and pour on the wine and lemon juice. Place the bay leaves and onion on top. Sprinkle on the bread crumbs and dot with butter. Cover and bake in a preheated 300° oven for 15 minutes. Meanwhile, toss the chopped dried fruits with the cinnamon and set aside. Uncover the casserole, raise the oven temperature to 400° and continue baking 5 minutes. Serve the eels with mashed potatoes and the dried fruit mixture.

Volendam is a small Dutch fishing village that tourists consider a kind of symbol of old Holland because the fishermen still wear wide pants and wooden shoes and the women wear beautiful white linen bonnets. But very few tourists will ever really know how Volendam stewed eel tastes, since the good people of Volendam prepare it mainly for their own tables.

Blankenbergse tong

Gebakken paling

Waterbaars

Sole Blankenberge style

4 servings

Sauce base:
- *1 cup water*
- *½ cup dry white wine or vermouth*
- *1 slice onion*
- *½ stalk celery, cut in 1 inch pieces*
- *1 slice lemon*
- *¼ teaspoon thyme*
- *1 bay leaf*
- *½ teaspoon salt*
- *5 peppercorns*
  Head and bones of the fish, if available

- *6 tablespoons butter*
- *1 medium sized onion, finely chopped*
- *2 tablespoons flour*
- *1 tablespoon prepared (Dijon type) mustard*
- *1½–2 pounds sole fillets*
- *¼ cup flour seasoned with ¼ teaspoon salt and Freshly ground black pepper*
- *2 tablespoons finely chopped parsley*

In a heavy saucepan, combine the ingredients for the sauce base. Bring to a boil, lower the heat and simmer slowly for 30 minutes. Strain the broth. Meanwhile, melt 2 tablespoons of the butter in another heavy saucepan and sauté the onion very slowly until tender. Do not allow it to brown. Stir in the 2 tablespoons flour and cook 1 minute. Add the strained broth gradually, stirring constantly until the sauce is thickened and smooth. Stir in the mustard.

Keep the sauce warm. Heat the remaining butter in a skillet until very hot. Roll the sole fillets in the seasoned flour and fry in the hot butter until golden brown on both sides. Place a few spoonfuls of sauce on a warm serving dish and arrange the fillets attractively on the sauce. Sprinkle with parsley. Serve immediately and pass the remaining sauce separately.

Baked eel

4 servings

- *2 pounds eel*
- *½ teaspoon salt*
- *1 egg, lightly beaten*
- *½ cup dry bread crumbs*
- *5 tablespoons butter*

Have the eel cleaned. Cut the eel into 2 inch pieces. Rub with salt and set aside for 5 minutes. Dip the pieces in the egg and then the bread crumbs. Heat the butter and fry the eel over high heat until browned (about 5 minutes). Cover and cook for another 15 to 20 minutes over low heat. Turn the fish occasionally. Serve with mayonnaise or a tomato sauce and a salad.

Fresh water bass

4 servings

- *4 cups water*
- *1 teaspoon salt*
- *2 parsley stems*
- *8 small (¼ pound) bass or perch, cleaned*
- *½ bunch fresh parsley*
- *4 thin slices white bread, buttered*
- *4 thin slices pumpernickel bread*
  Melted butter

Place the water, salt and parsley stems in a pan large enough to hold the fish comfortably. Bring to a boil and add the fish. Reduce the heat and poach the fish for 5 to 7 minutes. Meanwhile, cover the slices of buttered white bread with slices of pumpernickel. Trim the edges to match exactly, then cut into small squares. Garnish the fish with parsley sprigs and serve it in its cooking liquid accompanied by the squares of bread and melted butter.

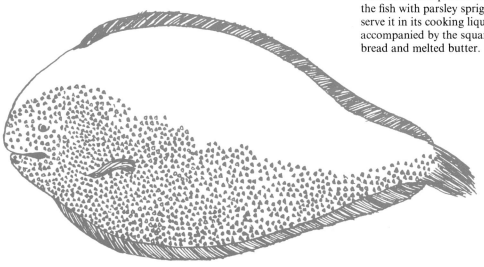

Brusselse karper

Carp Brussels style

4 servings

  1 *(2 pound) carp*
  6 *tablespoons vinegar*
  1 *small slice pork rind*
  2 *carrots, sliced*
  1 *leek or 1 medium sized*
     onion, sliced
  1 *stalk celery, sliced*
 ¼ *teaspoon thyme*
  1 *bay leaf*
  1 *sprig parsley*
  1 *cup beer*
 ½ *teaspoon salt*
     Freshly ground black pepper
  2 *teaspoons sugar*
     Dash of nutmeg
  1 *thick slice pound cake*
  2 *teaspoons honey*
 ¼ *teaspoon powdered ginger*
  1 *tablespoon cornstarch*
     dissolved in
     2 tablespoons cooking liquid
  3 *tablespoons butter*

Place the fish in just enough water to cover. Add vinegar and let stand for 1 hour. Drain the carp. Place pork rind, carrots, leek, celery, thyme, bay leaf and parsley in a pan. Place carp on top. Pour in the beer and enough water to just cover the fish. Sprinkle with salt, pepper, sugar and nutmeg. Bring to a boil and immediately lower the heat. Poach at a slow simmer for 30 minutes. Carefully remove fish and place on a warm dish. Remove pork rind, parsley and bay leaf. Add the pound cake, honey and ginger and let the pound cake soak until saturated. Strain and rub the solids through a sieve. Return the purée to

the sauce. Thicken the sauce with the cornstarch mixture. Swirl in the butter. Pour the sauce over the fish and serve.

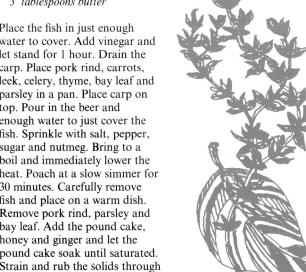

Truite à l'ardennaise

Trout Ardenne style

4 servings

  4 *whole trout (each about*
     ¾ pound)
  1 *cup white wine*
  1 *cup water*
  2 *carrots, peeled and sliced*
  1 *leek, sliced*
  1 *sprig parsley*
 ¼ *teaspoon thyme*
  1 *bay leaf*
  1 *clove*
 ½ *teaspoon salt*
  6 *peppercorns, crushed*
  2 *teaspoons cornstarch*
  3 *tablespoons butter, softened*
  1 *tablespoon finely chopped*
     parsley

Pour the wine into a pan and add the water, carrots, leek, parsley, thyme, bay leaf, clove, salt and peppercorns. Bring to a boil, lower the heat and simmer for 30 minutes. Poach the trout in this court bouillon for 6 to 10 minutes. Carefully remove the trout from the broth and place on a warm serving dish. Strain the broth, place over high heat and reduce to 1 cup. Thicken the liquid with the cornstarch dissolved in 2 tablespoons of cold water. Add the butter and beat it in with a wire whisk until the butter is dissolved. Pour the sauce over the trout and sprinkle with parsley.

Moules à la bruxelloise

Mussels Brussels style

4 servings

 10 *pounds mussels, cleaned and*
     brushed
  3 *tablespoons butter*
     Celery leaves from 1 bunch
     celery, chopped
 10 *sprigs parsley*
  1 *onion, chopped*
  1 *cup white wine*
     Freshly ground black pepper

Heat the butter in a large pan over low heat and add celery leaves, parsley, onion, wine and pepper. Add the mussels and cover the pan. Simmer until the shells open, 7 to 10 minutes. Strain the broth. Transfer the mussels and the broth to a warm serving dish and serve immediately.

Stews and casserole dishes

One old Dutch soldiers' song complains about the traditional army menu: stew, hard brown bread and beans. Soldiers now eat much better, of course, but beans still form a favorite part of the Dutch menu. Brown beans with bacon and sometimes molasses, white beans with a sour egg sauce and peas with bacon and mustard are all still part of traditional Dutch cooking. Bean soup is also popular: thick, hearty soup that sticks to the ribs and sometimes forms a complete meal. For many Dutchmen, the aroma of brown bean soup is the most hearty welcome-home imaginable on a cold winter's night.

Beans are used, in fact, in almost every possible way. During the war, for instance, when there was almost no meat available, the creative Dutch housewife ground white and brown beans and mixed them with herbs and spices to make a kind of hamburger.

The Dutch have a great fondness for vegetables and eat many fresh vegetables even in the middle of the winter. This traditional farmers' dish is a good example. It is called 'vijfschaft,' which means 'five kinds,' because it is made out of five different fruits and vegetables: beans, carrots, onions, apples and potatoes.

Vijfschaft

Brown beans with sausage

6 servings

- ½ pound kidney or pinto beans
- 2 pounds carrots, peeled and sliced
- 4 onions, cut into rings
- 2 green apples, peeled, cored and cut into wedges
- 2 pounds potatoes, peeled and thinly sliced
- 1 teaspoon salt
- 1 tablespoon cornstarch dissolved in 2 tablespoons water
- 4 tablespoons butter
- ½ pound sliced bacon, fried until crisp
- 1 large smoked sausage, sliced or
- 6 frankfurters

Soak the beans overnight in water to cover. Drain the beans and place in a heavy casserole large enough to hold all the vegetables. Cover the beans with water and bring to a boil. Lower the heat, cover and cook 1 hour. Add the carrots, onions and apples and simmer 15 minutes. Add the potatoes and salt and continue cooking 20 to 30 minutes or until the potatoes are tender. Stir in the cornstarch mixture to thicken the sauce. Swirl in the butter. Arrange the bacon and hot sausage on top of the vegetables and serve.

Raasdonders

Pea dish

4 servings

   1 pound pea beans or
      navy beans
   1 teaspoon salt
 ½ pound bacon, fried until crisp
   2 onions, sliced into rings and
      sautéed in butter until
      light brown
      Baked apple slices
   8 gherkins
      Pickled onions
      Sliced ham
      Boiled potatoes
   1 lemon, thinly sliced
      Mustard
      Catsup
      Piccallilly

Soak the pea beans overnight in
water to cover. Bring to a boil
in the soaking water, add the salt
and cook, covered, over low heat
for 1½ to 2 hours or until
tender. Drain the pea beans and
serve them on a platter
surrounded by various
condiments, such as crisp bacon
slices, sautéed onion rings,
baked apple slices, gherkins,
pickled onions, sliced ham,
boiled potatoes, lemon slices,
mustard, catsup and piccallilly.
In Holland this is a very
popular winter dish. Everyone
makes his choice of
accompaniments and serves
himself to taste. A good glass of
beer goes very well with this
dish.

Boerenkool met worst

Curly kale and sausage

4 servings

   3 pounds curly kale
   3 pounds potatoes, peeled
      and quartered
   1 pound smoked sausage or
      Frankfurters
   4 tablespoons butter
      Milk
      Freshly ground black pepper

Shred the kale very finely and
cook in 1 cup boiling salted
water for 40 minutes. Add
potatoes and sausage and more
water if necessary to prevent
burning. Cook 30 minutes more.
Remove sausage. Mash kale
and potatoes well and stir in
enough milk to make a smooth
purée. Season to taste with
pepper and more salt, if
necessary. Serve on a warm
platter and top with the sausage.
This dish is very popular in
Holland during winter. The
Dutch say that curly kale is at
its best as soon as the first frost
has passed.

Hete bliksem

Apples and potatoes

4 servings

   1 pound lean bacon in one
      piece, rind removed
 1½ pounds sweet apples, cored
      and quartered
 1½ pounds tart cooking apples,
      peeled, cored and quartered
   4 pounds potatoes, peeled and
      quartered

Cover the bacon with water and
cook for 30 minutes. Add
potatoes and apples and cook
for 30 minutes more. Remove
bacon from the pan and slice it.
Drain and mash the potatoes
and apples and place on a flat
serving dish. Top with the sliced
bacon.

Peren op de vleesketel

Pears with stewed meat

4 servings

  12 small pears
 ½ teaspoon tarragon
 1½ to 2 pounds beef (chuck)
   6 cups beef broth
   4 medium sized potatoes,
      peeled and cut into large
      chunks

Place the pears and tarragon in a
saucepan and add water to
cover. Simmer the pears,
covered, for 2 hours. Meanwhile,
cook the beef in the broth about
2 hours or until tender. Cook
the potatoes, covered, in boiling
salted water about 20 minutes or
until tender. Drain the pears and
arrange in the center of a
platter. Slice the meat and place
the slices around the pears.
Finally, arrange the potatoes
around the meat. Moisten with a
little of the broth or
pear-cooking liquid and pass
the rest separately.

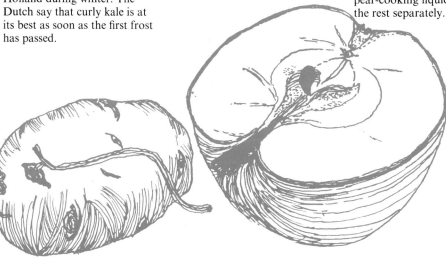

Leidse hutspot

Hotch potch Leiden style

4 servings

- 4 cups water
- 1 teaspoon salt
- 2 pounds lean beef (rump, round, etc.)
- 3 medium sized onions, cut into rings
- 3 large carrots, peeled and sliced
- 4 medium sized potatoes, peeled and cubed
- 4 tablespoons butter, softened
  Freshly ground black pepper

Bring the water to a boil. Add the salt and beef, cover and simmer over low heat for 1½ hours. Add the vegetables and continue to simmer 45 minutes. Remove the meat from the pan and keep warm. Drain and mash the vegetables. Add the butter, pepper and more salt, if necessary, and mix well. Place the mashed vegetables on a serving platter. Slice the meat and arrange on top. Serve immediately.

Gentse hutspot

Stew from Ghent

4 servings

- 1 pound boneless beef shank
- ½ pound pigs' feet (opt.)
- ¼ pound bacon in 1 piece
- 4 cups water
- 1 teaspoon salt
  Freshly ground black pepper
- 2 bay leaves
- 2 cloves
- 3 medium sized carrots, peeled and sliced
- 2 leeks, sliced
- 2 large stalks celery, sliced
- ½ small cabbage, shredded
- 3 medium sized potatoes, peeled and quartered

Place the beef, pigs' feet, bacon, water, salt, pepper, bay leaves and cloves in a heavy pan and bring to a boil. Skim the broth, lower the heat, cover and simmer 3 hours. Add the carrots, leeks, and celery and simmer 30 minutes. Add cabbage and potatoes and simmer until potatoes are tender. Discard pigs' feet if used. Slice the beef and bacon and arrange meats and vegetables on a platter. Serve the broth separately.

Hutspot van kalfsborst

Veal breast stew

6 servings

- ¼ pound bacon, diced
- 2 pounds breast of veal
- 6 cups water
- 3 large carrots, peeled and sliced
- 2 medium sized onions, sliced
- 1 stalk celery, sliced
- 4 turnips, cubed
- 2 sprigs parsley
- 1 clove garlic, crushed
- 1 bay leaf
- ½ teaspoon salt
  Freshly ground black pepper

Fry the bacon in a heavy casserole until crisp. Remove bacon and drain on paper towels. Cut the veal into large pieces and brown in the bacon fat. Pour off all the accumulated fat. Add all the remaining ingredients and the drained bacon and bring to a boil. Lower the heat, cover and simmer slowly 2 hours. Arrange the meat and vegetables on a warm platter. Reduce the broth over high heat to 2 cups. Strain and serve separately in a sauce dish.

Jachtschotel

Hunters' stew

4 servings

- 2 pounds lean beef (rump, round, etc.), cubed
- ½ cup flour seasoned with ½ teaspoon salt
  Freshly ground black pepper
- 3 tablespoons butter
- 2 medium sized onions, finely chopped
- 1 cooking apple, peeled, cored and finely chopped
- ½ cup red wine
- ¾ cup beef broth
- 2 bay leaves
- 4 peppercorns, crushed
- 4 juniper berries, crushed
- 2 cloves
- 4 medium sized potatoes, peeled, boiled and mashed
- 2 tablespoons butter, melted

Roll the beef cubes in seasoned flour. Heat the butter in a heavy casserole. Add the beef cubes and brown quickly over high heat. Add the onions and apple and cook for 3 to 4 minutes over medium heat. Add wine and broth and cook for a few minutes, scraping up the brown bits clinging to the bottom of the pan. Add the bay leaves, peppercorns, juniper berries and cloves. Reduce the heat, cover and simmer slowly 1½ hours or until the beef is tender. Strain the sauce and place the meat and vegetables in a shallow ovenproof serving dish. Spread the mashed potatoes in a layer on top of the meat and pour on the melted butter. Bake in a preheated 425° oven for 15 minutes or until the potatoes are brown.

Sauerkraut. North of Amsterdam, there is a region covered with cabbage fields as far as the eye can see. Here small wooden boats loaded with cabbages make their way through the narrow canals to the sauerkraut processing plants.

Zuurkoolschotel

Sauerkraut

4 servings

1½ pounds sauerkraut
    Small piece of bacon rind
  4 juniper berries, crushed
½ pound fat bacon, in 1 piece
  4 thick slices uncooked ham
¾ cup white wine
  8 thin slices lean bacon
  4 frankfurters
  2 pounds small potatoes,
    peeled and cooked

Place the bacon rind in a heavy pan and spread the sauerkraut and the juniper berries over the bacon rind. Place the fat bacon in the center of the sauerkraut and arrange ham around it. Pour wine over the sauerkraut and cover with the thin slices of lean bacon. Cook, covered, for 1 hour over low heat. Add the frankfurters and sausage and simmer for another 20 minutes. Arrange the sauerkraut on a warm, flat dish. Slice the fat bacon and arrange on top. Garnish the dish with the ham, frankfurters, sliced sausage, whole potatoes and thinly sliced lean bacon. Serve with melted butter.

Stew from Ghent (recipe page 43, 2nd column)

Nassi goreng

Nassi goreng is one of Holland's favorite dishes. It is a fried rice dish with vegetables, pieces of meat, hot Indonesian spices and a fried egg on top. Nassi goreng is eaten once a week by many families, and in the Dutch navy, Wednesday is always nassi goreng day. The dish came from Indonesia, when the East Indies were a Dutch colony. It began as a meal made from leftovers, created by ingenious Indonesian cooks who prepared it from everything left over from a complicated set of rice dishes prepared the day before. Dry rice was fried together with what remained of the chicken, meat, shrimp and vegetables. Nassi goreng is in fact called a 'pyjama' dish in Indonesia because it would be embarassing to serve it to a guest. In Holland, however, nassi goreng is a favorite home-cooked meal and a popular dish in many Chinese and Indonesian restaurants where it is also available to be taken home. Nassi goreng first became popular with the Dutch who once lived in Indonesia and returned to Holland to find Dutch cooking rather bland. Their taste for a good, spicy nassi goreng was later adopted by everyone.

Indonesian baked rice

4 servings

- 2 cups raw rice
- 4 tablespoons oil
- ¾ pound lean pork, cubed
- 2 onions, chopped
- 2 cloves garlic, crushed
- 1 teaspoon salt
  Freshly ground black pepper
- 1 teaspoon sambal
- 1 teaspoon powdered ginger
- 1 teaspoon laos, ketoembar or trassi (*Indonesian spices*), optional
- 2 leeks, cut into rings
- ½ cup baby shrimp, peeled
- 1 tablespoon ketjap or soy sauce
- 2 tablespoons finely chopped celery tops
- 2 eggs
- 2 tomatoes, sliced
- 4 gherkins, sliced

Cook the rice according to the package directions and set aside to cool. Heat the oil in a heavy saucepan and brown the meat quickly over high heat. Add onions, garlic, salt, pepper and spices and sauté for 5 minutes. Add leeks and sauté another 2 minutes. Add the cold rice and cook for a few minutes over high heat, stirring constantly. Add shrimp, ketjap or soy sauce and celery greens and heat through. In the meantime, make an omelet with the 2 eggs and cut into long strips. Serve the nassi goreng on a warm platter and garnish with the strips of omelet, sliced tomatoes and the gherkins. Serve a cool glass of beer with this dish.

Meat dishes

Hollandse biefstuk

Dutch steak

4 servings

- 4 small steaks (fillet, shell, etc.)
- 1 teaspoon salt
  Freshly ground black pepper
- 3 tablespoons butter
- 2 tablespoons milk

Rub the steaks on both sides with salt and pepper. Heat the butter until very hot and sauté the steaks on each side for a few minutes until they reach the desired degree of doneness. Remove the steaks from the pan and keep warm. Add the milk to the pan and stir up the brown bits clinging to the bottom. Pour the sauce over the steaks and serve. Dutch steaks are always served with fried potatoes and fresh green peas.

Vlaamse biefstuk

Flemish steak

4 servings

- 4 tablespoons marrow
- 4 tablespoons butter
- 4 shallots or scallions, finely chopped
- 2 tablespoons finely chopped parsley
- ½ teaspoon salt
  Freshly ground black pepper
  Juice of ½ lemon
- 4 rib eye or sirloin steaks

Ask the butcher for a few marrow bones sawed into 1½ to 2 inch pieces. Have the bones at room temperature and run a sharp knife between bone and marrow. The marrow will push out of the bones easily. Blanch the marrow in boiling water for 3 minutes and chop it finely. Melt 1 tablespoon butter in a small skillet. Sauté the shallots over low heat until tender but not brown. Add the marrow, parsley, salt, pepper and lemon juice. Keep warm while preparing the steaks. Melt the remaining butter in a large sauté pan or skillet. When the butter is very hot, add the steaks and sauté over high heat for a few minutes on each side or until they reach the desired degree of doneness. Top each steak with some of the shallot mixture and serve with potato chips (French fried potatoes).

Gehaktballen

Meat balls

4 servings

- ½ pound ground beef
- ½ pound ground pork
- 4 slices day-old bread, crusts removed
- ½ cup milk
- 6 tablespoons butter
- ½ onion, finely chopped
- ½ teaspoon salt
  Freshly ground black pepper
  Dash of nutmeg
- ½ cup fine dry breadcrumbs
- ½ cup beef broth
- 1 teaspoon tomato paste

Combine the meats. Soak the bread in the milk. Heat 2 tablespoons butter and sauté the onion for 2 minutes. Squeeze the bread slices as dry as possible and crumble. Combine meat, bread, salt, pepper, nutmeg and onion and knead together. Form into 8 balls. Coat with bread crumbs. Heat the remaining butter and sauté the meat balls until brown on all sides. Pour out the butter, add the broth and simmer for 15 minutes. Remove meat balls from the pan. Add tomato paste to the broth and serve the broth separately with the meatballs and boiled potatoes.

Fricadelles à la bière

Meatballs with beer

4 servings

- 1 thick slice bread, crusts removed
- 3 tablespoons milk
- 1 pound ground beef
- ½ pound ground pork
- 1 egg
- ¼ teaspoon salt
  Freshly ground black pepper
- ½ teaspoon nutmeg
- 5 tablespoons butter, softened
- 2 cups beer
- 4 tablespoons flour

Soak the bread in the milk and then knead into the meat together with the egg, salt, pepper and nutmeg. Form 8 balls and sauté in 3 tablespoons butter until golden brown. Add the beer, cover the pan and simmer 20 minutes over very low heat. Cream the remaining 2 tablespoons butter with the flour. Add the flour mixture bit by bit, stirring constantly with a wire whisk until a thick sauce is formed.

Gestoofde runderlappen

Stewed beef

4 servings

1½–2 pounds beef (rump, shoulder, etc.) cut into 4 pieces
1 teaspoon salt
Freshly ground black pepper
3 tablespoons bacon fat or oil
1 large onion, sliced
1 bay leaf
2 cloves
6 peppercorns, crushed
1 tablespoon vinegar
1 tablespoon prepared (Dijon type) mustard
Water

Rub the beef on all sides with salt and pepper. Heat the bacon fat in a heavy casserole and brown the beef quickly on all sides over high heat. Add and sauté the onion during the last few minutes of browning the beef. Add the remaining ingredients, using only enough water to barely cover the beef. Bring to a boil, reduce the heat and cover the pan. Simmer slowly for 2 to 3 hours, turning the meat every 30 minutes. The meat should be very tender. Serve with red cabbage and mashed potatoes.

Vlaamse osselappen

Flemish beef

4 servings

1¼ pounds flank steak
3 tablespoons butter
2 onions, thinly sliced
3 tablespoons flour
2 cups beer
1 bay leaf
1 teaspoon thyme
1 sprig parsley
2 teaspoons sugar
1 tablespoon vinegar
1 teaspoon salt
Freshly ground black pepper
1 slice white bread, crusts removed
1 tablespoon prepared (Dijon type) mustard

Cut the flank steak into pieces and brown lightly in the butter over high heat. Remove the meat from the pan. Sauté the onions in the same butter. Add the flour and cook until light brown. Gradually add the beer, stirring constantly until the sauce is thickened and smooth. Add the meat, bay leaf, thyme, parsley, sugar, vinegar, salt and pepper. Cover the pan and let the meat simmer slowly for 1 hour. Spread the slice of bread with mustard and place the bread in the pan. Simmer for 1 hour more.

Hachee

Dutch hash

4 servings

1½ to 2 pounds lean boneless beef, pork or veal, diced
1 teaspoon salt
Freshly ground black pepper
4 tablespoons butter
2 large onions, cut into rings
5 tablespoons flour
3 cups beef broth
2 bay leaves
2 cloves
1 teaspoon sugar
2 tablespoons vinegar

Toss the diced meat with salt and pepper. Heat the butter and sauté the meat and onions over high heat until lightly browned. Add the flour and cook, stirring, 2 minutes. Add the broth gradually, stirring up the brown bits clinging to the bottom of the pan. Add the remaining ingredients, cover and simmer slowly 1½ hours. Serve with rice or boiled potatoes.

Gentse stoverij

Casserole from Ghent

4 servings

½–¾ pound veal kidneys
½–¾ pound calves' liver
2 tablespoons butter
2 onions, finely chopped
1 cup water
½ teaspoon salt
Freshly ground black pepper
1 bay leaf
½ teaspoon thyme
½ cup beer
1 slice white bread spread with 1 tablespoon mustard
1 tablespoon vinegar
1 tablespoon cornstarch dissolved in 1 tablespoon water

Simmer the kidneys in boiling water for 8 minutes. Cut liver and kidneys into pieces. Heat the butter and sauté the onions until golden brown. Add the meats, water, salt, pepper, bay leaf and thyme. Simmer, covered, for 1 hour. Add the beer and the bread and simmer for another 30 minutes. Remove the meat from the pan and keep warm on a serving dish. Strain the sauce, forcing the onions and bread through a sieve and add vinegar. Stir in cornstarch mixture to thicken the sauce. Pour the sauce over the meat. Serve with boiled potatoes.

Rollade

Collared beef

8 servings

    2 pounds sirloin steak in
       1 piece
    1 teaspoon salt
       Freshly ground black pepper
    1 pound filet mignon steak in
       1 piece
    4 tablespoons butter
    ½ teaspoon thyme
    1 onion, finely chopped
    1 bay leaf
    1 cup milk

Have the sirloin steak flattened to a thickness of ½ inch. Rub the meat with salt and pepper. Place the filet mignon steak over the sirloin steak, roll up and tie in several places. Heat the butter in a heavy casserole until very hot. Brown the meat quickly on all sides over high heat. Lower the heat and add thyme, onion and bay leaf. Cover the pan and simmer for 1½ hours, turning occasionally. Add a bit of butter now and then if the meat tends to stick. Remove the meat from the pan and cool slightly before slicing. Remove the bay leaf and add the milk, stirring up the brown bits clinging to the bottom of the pan. Serve the sliced rollade on a warm platter and pass the sauce separately. Serve mashed potatoes and fresh vegetables with this dish.

Slavinken

Ground pork rolls

4 servings

    2 slices day-old bread,
       crusts removed
    ¼ cup milk
    1 pound ground pork or
       sausage meat
    ½ teaspoon salt
       Freshly ground black pepper
       Dash of nutmeg
    ½ onion, finely chopped
    8 thin slices lean bacon
    2 tablespoons butter
    ½ cup milk

Crumble the bread and soak in ¼ cup milk. Squeeze bread as dry as possible and combine with ground pork or sausage meat, salt, pepper, nutmeg and onion. Knead mixture until well blended. Form 4 cylinders, 3″ long and wrap 2 slices bacon around each cylinder cross-wise. Tie at intervals with thread to secure the bacon. Heat butter in a frying pan and fry the cylinders over medium heat 8 minutes. Turn and fry another 8 minutes. Remove the meat from the pan and keep warm. Pour out the accumulated fat. Add the milk to the pan and cook over high heat scraping up the brown bits clinging to the bottom. Serve the pork rolls with mashed potatoes and a salad and pass the milk gravy separately.

Pork chops with apricots

Ground pork rolls are called 'slavinken' in Dutch. The word literally means 'salad birds' *because the small rolls suggest the form of a small roasted bird and are eaten in the fall with a tender, fresh lettuce salad.*

Varkenslapjes met abrikozen

Pork chops with apricots

4 servings

    4 thick pork chops
 ¼ teaspoon powdered ginger
    1 teaspoon salt
       Freshly ground black pepper
    2 tablespoons butter
    2 small onions, finely chopped
    1 teaspoon tomato paste
 ½ cup red wine
    8 canned apricot halves
    3 tablespoons fine dry
       breadcrumbs
    1 tablespoon butter

Season the chops with ginger, salt and pepper. Fry the chops in the butter over high heat until evenly browned. Place the chops in an ovenproof dish and surround with the chopped onions. Discard the fat from the frying pan and add the tomato paste and wine. Pour this mixture over the pork chops. Cover with apricot halves, sprinkle with breadcrumbs and dot with butter. Cook in a preheated 325° oven for 45 minutes. Serve with rice and green beans.

Kalfstong met zure saus

Veal tongue with sour sauce

6 servings

    1 *veal tongue (about 3 pounds)*
    1 *teaspoon salt*
    1 *carrot, peeled and sliced*
    1 *onion, sliced*
    Leafy tops from 1 bunch celery
    1 *sprig parsley*
  ¼ *teaspoon mace*
    4 *peppercorns, crushed*
    1 *clove*
    1 *bay leaf*

For the sauce:
    4 *tablespoons butter*
    4 *tablespoons flour*
    2 *cups cooking liquid*
    2 *eggs*
    3 *tablespoons wine vinegar*

Soak the tongue in cold water for several hours. Rinse the tongue under cold running water and rub lightly with salt. Place in a pan with water to cover and add the vegetables, herbs and spices. Bring to a boil and cook over low heat for about 3 hours or until tender. Remove the tongue from the pan and remove the skin. Strain the cooking liquid and reserve 2 cups for the sauce. Keep the tongue warm in the remaining cooking liquid. Melt half of the butter, stir in the flour, and add the cooking liquid, stirring constantly until a smooth sauce is formed. Combine the eggs with a little of the warm sauce and add this mixture to the sauce, stirring constantly. Then, over very low heat, add the remaining butter and vinegar stirring constantly. Do not allow the sauce to boil after the eggs are added. Slice the tongue, arrange on a warm dish and serve lima beans and the sauce separately.

Filet de porc à l'escavèche

Marinated fillet of pork

6 servings

For the marinade:
  ¾ *cup white wine*
  ¾ *cup vinegar*
    1 *teaspoon thyme*
    2 *bay leaves*
    1 *clove garlic, crushed*
  ½ *teaspoon dried tarragon*
    6 *juniper berries, crushed*

    2 *pounds fillet of pork, 1 piece*
    2 *tablespoons oil*
    2 *medium sized carrots, peeled and sliced*
    1 *medium sized onion, sliced*
    1 *stalk celery, sliced*
    1 *sweet red or green pepper, seeded and cut into strips*
    1 *tablespoon chopped parsley*
    1 *pound tomatoes, peeled, seeded and sliced*
    2 *cloves garlic, crushed*
    1 *teaspoon salt*
    Freshly ground black pepper
    2 *tablespoons butter*

Combine marinade ingredients. Add pork and marinate overnight. Heat oil in a skillet and sauté carrots, onion, celery, red pepper and parsley for 5 minutes. Add tomatoes, garlic, salt and pepper and cook 2 minutes. Strain and add marinade and simmer 20 minutes. Meanwhile heat butter in a heavy casserole. Dry pork well with paper towels and brown on all sides in hot butter. Add vegetable mixture and bring to a simmer. Cover and cook 45 minutes to 1 hour or until pork is tender. Slice pork and serve vegetables separately.

Côtelettes de porc à la liégeoise

Pork chops from Liège

4 servings

    4 *pork chops*
  ½ *teaspoon salt*
    2 *juniper berries, finely crushed*
  ¼ *cup flour*
 1½ *tablespoons butter*
    1 *tablespoon oil*

Season the pork chops with the salt and juniper berries. Dredge the chops in the flour. Sauté in hot combined butter and oil until tender and golden brown on both sides.

Lever met spek en uien

Liver with bacon and onions

4 servings

>   8 *slices bacon*
>   1 *large onion, finely chopped*
>   4 *thin slices calves' liver*
>   ½ *teaspoon salt*
>   *Freshly ground black pepper*

Fry bacon until crisp. Drain on paper towels and keep warm. Sauté the onion in the rendered bacon fat until golden. Remove from the pan with a slotted spoon and keep warm. Sprinkle the liver with salt and pepper. In the same fat, brown the liver 3 to 4 minutes on each side. Transfer to a serving dish and cover with the bacon and onions. Serve with applesauce and mashed potatoes.

Foie de porc de Tournai

Pork liver Tournai style

6 servings

>   2 *pounds pork or beef liver*
>   1 *teaspoon salt*
>   *Freshly ground black pepper*
>   3 *tablespoons bacon fat or oil*
>   1 *medium sized onion,*
>   *thinly sliced*
>   3 *cups beef broth*
>   1 *teaspoon thyme*
>   1 *bay leaf*
>   1 *tablespoon sugar*
>   3 *tablespoons flour*
>   3 *tablespoons butter, softened*

Sprinkle the liver with salt and pepper. Heat the bacon fat until very hot and brown the liver quickly. Remove liver from the pan and sauté the onion in the same fat over medium heat. Return liver to the pan and add the broth, thyme, bay leaf and sugar. Cover and simmer over low heat 25 to 30 minutes until liver is tender. In a small bowl, blend the flour into the softened butter. Remove liver from the pan and keep warm. Reduce the broth to half its original quantity. With a wire whisk, beat the butter-flour mixture into the broth bit by bit until the sauce is thickened and smooth. Slice the liver and pour the thick sauce over. Serve immediately.

L'Atte

Pork from Ath

6 servings

>   2 to 2½ *pounds boneless*
>   *loin of pork**
>   2 *cloves garlic, cut into slivers*
>   4 *whole cloves*
>   *Coarse salt*
>   2 *bay leaves, crushed*
>   1 *teaspoon thyme*
>   3 *cups beef broth*

Make deep incisions all over the pork and insert the garlic slivers and cloves in the incisions. Rub the salt, bay leaves and thyme all over the surface of the pork. Place the pork in a shallow dish, cover with aluminum foil or plastic wrap and refrigerate 4 days. Wipe as much salt as possible from the pork and place in an ovenproof casserole. Pour in the broth. Bake in a preheated 350° oven for 1½ to 2 hours or until the pork is done and tender. Serve cold, in thin slices.

* Traditionally, pork breast is used for this dish, but it is not usually available in America so we have substituted pork loin.

Lever met pruimen

Liver with prunes

4 servings

>   ½ *pound dried pitted prunes*
>   1 *strip lemon rind*
>   ¼ *cup sugar*
>   2 *tablespoons bacon fat or*
>   *butter*
>   1 *large onion, thinly sliced*
>   1¼ *pounds calves' liver, diced*
>   1 *tablespoon flour*
>   1 *cup beef broth*
>   2 *tablespoons vinegar*
>   ½ *teaspoon salt*
>   *Freshly ground black pepper*
>   ½ *teaspoon thyme*
>   1 *bay leaf*

Soak prunes overnight in cold water. Drain. Barely cover with water, add lemon rind and sugar and simmer 5 to 10 minutes. In a large skillet, heat the bacon fat and sauté the onion over medium heat until light brown. Add the liver and sauté 3 minutes. Sprinkle on the flour and cook 1 to 2 minutes. Add the broth, stirring to scrape up the brown bits clinging to the pan. Add the remaining ingredients and the prunes with their liquid. Simmer 15 minutes and serve.

Foie de veau au vin rouge

Calves' liver with red wine

4 servings

½ teaspoon salt
   Freshly ground black pepper
1 bay leaf, crumbled
1 teaspoon thyme
1 tablespoon flour
1¼ pounds calves' liver, in
   1 piece
2 tablespoons butter
1 onion, finely chopped
1½ cups dry red wine
2 tablespoons sugar

Combine the salt, pepper,
bay leaf, thyme and flour and
rub into the liver. Heat the
butter and sauté the liver and
onions over moderately high
heat until liver is brown.
Add the wine and sugar.
Reduce heat, cover and simmer
slowly for 1 hour. Slice the
liver and arrange on a warm
serving dish. Cook the liquid
over high heat until reduced by
half. Strain and pour over the
sliced liver.

Varkenshaasje in roomsaus

Pork fillets with cream sauce

4 servings

1½ pounds pork fillets cut
   from the loin
1 teaspoon salt
   Freshly ground black pepper
3 tablespoons butter
1 small onion, finely chopped
½ cup sliced mushrooms
½ cup white wine
2 tablespoons flour
¾ cup cream, heated

Season the pork fillets with salt
and pepper. Heat the butter
and brown the meat 8 minutes
on both sides. Remove the meat
and keep warm. Sauté the
onion and the mushrooms in
the same butter for 2 minutes.
Add wine and simmer, covered,
for 10 minutes. Combine the
flour with 4 tablespoons cream.
Add the remaining cream to
the pan. Add the flour mixture,
stirring constantly, until the
sauce is smooth. Cover the
fillets with a little of the sauce
and pass the rest separately.

Ox tongue is as popular in Holland as it is in Belgium. It is always a hit and so easy to make that even the most inexperienced housewife can prepare it (recipe page 54).

Rognons à la liégeoise

Kidneys Liège style

4 servings

1½ *pounds veal kidneys*
  1 *teaspoon salt*
    Freshly ground black pepper
  8 *juniper berries, finely crushed*
  3 *tablespoons butter*
 ½ *cup hot water*
  2 *slices white bread, crusts removed*
  1 *tablespoon butter*

Simmer kidneys in boiling salted water for 8 minutes. Rinse well under cold running water and dry thoroughly. Mix the salt, pepper and juniper berries and rub the kidneys with this mixture. Heat the 3 tablespoons butter and sauté the kidneys 15 minutes over low heat. Add water, cover and simmer 10 minutes. Cut each slice of bread into 4 squares and sauté in 1 tablespoon hot butter until brown on both sides. Slice kidneys and serve on toasted bread.

Ossetong met rozijnesaus

Ox tongue with raisin sauce

8 servings

- 1 *ox tongue (4 pounds)*
- 1 *teaspoon salt*
- 1 *carrot, peeled and sliced*
- 1 *onion, sliced*
  Few celery tops
- 1 *sprig parsley*
- 6 *peppercorns, crushed*
- 1 *bay leaf*
- 1 *clove*

Soak the tongue for at least 3 hours in cold water. Rinse under cold running water. Combine the remaining ingredients in a large pot. Add the tongue and cover with water. Bring to a boil, cover and simmer gently for at least 3 hours or until meat is tender. Remove the skin from the tongue and cut the meat into slices $\frac{1}{2}$ inch thick. Keep warm. Strain liquid and reserve $2\frac{1}{2}$ cups for the sauce. Serve with rice or mashed potatoes, assorted vegetables and a raisin sauce.

For the sauce:
- $\frac{1}{2}$ *cup seedless raisins*
- $\frac{1}{2}$ *cup red port wine*
- 3 *tablespoons butter*
- 3 *tablespoons flour*
- $2\frac{1}{2}$ *cups cooking liquid*
- 1 *tablespoon tomato purée*
- $\frac{1}{4}$ *teaspoon sugar*
- $\frac{1}{2}$ *teaspoon vinegar*
  Salt
  Freshly ground pepper

Soak the raisins in the port for at least 1 hour. Heat the butter and stir in flour. Gradually add the reserved cooking liquid, stirring constantly until a smooth sauce is formed. Strain raisins and add the port, tomato purée, sugar and vinegar to the sauce. Reduce sauce over medium heat to $\frac{2}{3}$ its original quantity. Add raisins, season to taste with salt and pepper and simmer for a few minutes.

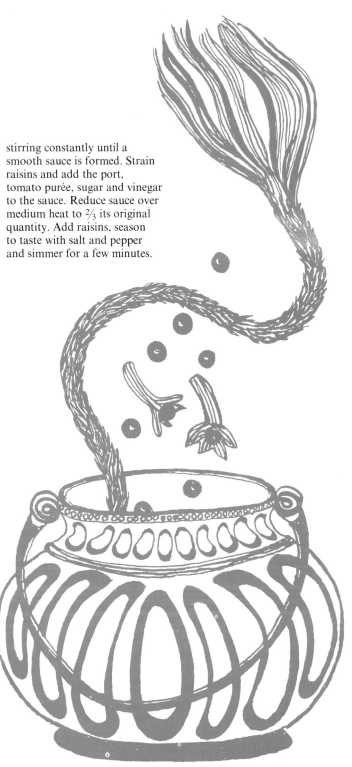

Vlaamse ossestaart

Flemish oxtail

4 servings

- 1 *oxtail, cut into pieces at the joints*
- 2 *cloves*
- 4 *juniper berries, crushed*
- 1 *onion*
- 4 *cups water*
- $\frac{1}{2}$ *teaspoon salt*
  Freshly ground black pepper
- 3 *medium sized carrots, peeled and sliced*
- 2 *stalks celery, sliced*
- $\frac{1}{4}$ *small cabbage, shredded*
- $\frac{1}{2}$ *pound lean bacon, in 1 piece*
- 1 *pound potatoes, peeled and cubed*
- 1 *garlic sausage*

Soak the oxtail in boiling water for 5 minutes and rinse under cold, running water. Tie the cloves, juniper berries and onion in a cheesecloth bag. Place the water in a heavy pan, bring to a boil and add the oxtail, ingredients in the cheesecloth, salt and pepper. Cover and simmer 2 hours. Add carrots, celery, cabbage and bacon and simmer, covered, 1 hour. Add potatoes and cook, covered, 30 minutes more. Add the sausage during the last 10 minutes of cooking time. Discard cheesecloth bag. Remove the vegetables with a slotted spoon and place on a serving dish. Slice the bacon and sausage and arrange them and the oxtail on top of the vegetables. Serve immediately.

Ragoût de mouton à l'ardennaise

Lamsvlees met rijst

Lamb stew from the Ardennes

4 servings

  2 *tablespoons butter*
$1\frac{1}{2}$–2 *pounds boneless leg of*
    lamb, cubed
  2 *cups water*
  1 *clove garlic, crushed*
  3 *medium sized carrots,*
    peeled and sliced
  2 *turnips, cubed*
  1 *onion, sliced*
  $\frac{1}{4}$ *small cabbage, shredded*
  1 *teaspoon salt*
    Freshly ground black pepper
  4 *medium sized potatoes,*
    peeled and thinly sliced

Melt the butter in a heavy casserole and sauté the lamb over high heat until brown. Add the water, garlic, carrots, turnips, onion, cabbage, salt and pepper and bring to a boil. Lower the heat, cover and simmer $1\frac{1}{2}$ hours. Add the potatoes, cover and simmer 30 minutes more. Serve from the casserole.

Lamb with rice

4 servings

  3 *tablespoons butter*
$1\frac{1}{2}$ *pounds boneless leg of lamb,*
    cut into 1 inch cubes
  1 *large onion, coarsely chopped*
  2 *cups water*
  1 *bay leaf*
  1 *teaspoon thyme*
  1 *tablespoon finely chopped*
    parsley
  1 *teaspoon salt*
    Freshly ground black pepper
    Dash of nutmeg
  1 *cup rice*

Melt the butter in a heavy casserole and sauté the lamb and onion over high heat until nicely browned. Add the remaining ingredients except the rice and bring to a boil. Lower the heat, cover and simmer slowly for $1\frac{1}{2}$ hours. Add the rice and stir once with a fork. Cover and simmer 30 minutes more or until the rice has absorbed the liquid and is tender. Serve from the casserole.

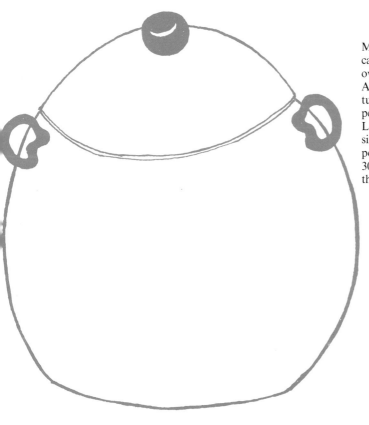

Poultry and game dishes

Belgian chicken stew is the great speciality of the ancient city of Ghent in Flanders. It is the favorite dish of the Belgian King, Baudouin.

Waterzooi van kip

Belgian chicken stew

4 servings

- 1 (3 pound) roasting chicken
  Salt
  Freshly ground black pepper
- 3 tablespoons butter
- 1 leek, finely chopped
- 1 stalk celery, finely chopped
- 1 onion, finely chopped
- 1 carrot, peeled and finely
  chopped
- 2 tablespoons finely chopped
  parsley
- ¾ cup chicken broth
- 2 egg yolks
- 2 tablespoons finely chopped
  parsley for garnish

Cut the chicken into 8 pieces and rub each piece with salt and pepper. Butter the bottom of a heavy casserole and make a layer of leek, celery, onion, carrot and parsley. Arrange the chicken pieces on top and place the pan over low heat for 10 minutes. Pour in the hot broth, cover the pan and simmer 1 hour. Remove the pieces of chicken. Beat the egg yolks lightly and add to the broth and the vegetables, stirring constantly. Place part of the mixture in shallow soup bowls. Top with the pieces of chicken and sprinkle with finely chopped parsley.

Brusselse kipgalantine

Chicken pâté

6 to 8 servings

- 4 cups water
- 1 sprig parsley
- ½ cup leafy celery tops
- ½ teaspoon salt
- 1 bay leaf
- ¼ teaspoon thyme
- 1 (1½ pound) chicken
- ½ pound ground pork
- ½ pound ground veal
- 1 clove garlic, crushed
- 1 small onion, finely chopped
- 2 eggs
- 3 tablespoons brandy
- ¼ pound sliced bacon

For the pastry:
- 1½ cups flour
  Pinch of salt
- 5 tablespoons butter
- 4 tablespoons ice water

- 1 egg yolk
- 1 tablespoon cream

Place the water, parsley, celery tops, salt, bay leaf and thyme in a heavy pan and bring to a boil. Lower the heat, add the chicken and simmer slowly for 1 hour. Meanwhile, prepare the pastry; place the flour and salt in a mixing bowl. Cut the butter into the flour with a pastry blender or 2 knives until the mixture resembles coarse meal. Add the water and stir with a fork until the dough can be gathered into a ball. Wrap the dough in wax paper and refrigerate 1 hour. When the chicken is cooked, drain it and remove the skin and bones. Cut the large pieces into strips and chop the remainder

finely. Combine the ground chicken with the pork, veal, garlic, onion, eggs and brandy. Line a pâté mold with the bacon strips and add the ground meat mixture. Arrange the strips of chicken on top lengthwise. Roll out the pastry and cover the pâté. Brush the top with lightly beaten egg yolk combined with 1 tablespoon cream. Make a funnel from aluminum foil and insert into the center of the pâté. Bake the pâté for 1 hour in a preheated 375° oven. Lower the oven temperature to 325°, cover the pâté with foil and bake 1 hour more. The pâté may be served warm or cold and should be sliced very thinly.

Kip met kerrierijst

Chicken and curry rice

4 servings

- 1 (3½ pound) chicken, cut
  into serving pieces
- 1 carrot, peeled and sliced
- 1 onion, finely chopped
- 1 sprig parsley
- 1 bay leaf
- ¼ teaspoon mace
- 1 teaspoon salt
- 4 peppercorns, crushed
- 1 cup rice
- 1 tablespoon curry powder

For the sauce:
- 3 tablespoons butter
- 4 tablespoons flour
- 3 cups reserved chicken broth
- ¼ cup tomato purée

Place chicken, carrot, onion, parsley, bay leaf, mace, salt and peppercorns in a heavy pan. Add water to cover and bring to a boil. Lower heat, cover and cook for 45 minutes to 1 hour or until chicken is tender. Meanwhile, cook the rice according to package directions. Stir the curry powder into the rice halfway through the cooking time. Remove the chicken pieces and keep warm. Strain and reserve the broth. Heat the butter in a saucepan. Stir in the flour and cook 2 minutes. Add 3 cups of broth gradually, stirring constantly until sauce is thickened and smooth. Stir in tomato purée. Rinse a ring mold with cold water and pack rice into mold. Insert rice on a warm platter and arrange chicken pieces in center.

Gans met appel

Goose with apples

8 servings

8 medium sized cooking apples
5 tablespoons butter
2 tablespoons brown sugar
2 teaspoons cinnamon
4 cups freshly made
   breadcrumbs
1 (9 to 10 pound) young
   goose or
2 (4 to 5 pound) ducks
1 teaspoon salt

Peel, core and chop the apples.
Heat the butter in a large skillet
and sauté the apples until
lightly browned. Add the sugar,
cinnamon and breadcrumbs and
cook, stirring, for 2 minutes.
Dry the goose thoroughly inside
and out and sprinkle the cavity
with salt. Stuff the goose with
the apple mixture and truss.
Prick the skin of the goose or
ducks all over with a fork to
allow the fat to drain off while
cooking. Place the goose on a
rack in a roasting pan and roast
breast side up in a preheated
400° oven for 15 minutes.
Reduce the heat to 350°, turn
the bird on its side and roast
50 minutes to 1 hour. Turn the
bird onto the other side and
roast another 50 minutes to
1 hour. Turn breast side up for
the last 15 minutes roasting
time. It will take 2¼ to 2½
hours total time for the goose to
cook. The ducks will be done in
about 1½ hours. Follow the
same procedure for roasting the
ducks but roast on each side
30 minutes only. Place the goose
on a serving platter, remove
trussing strings and let stand
10 to 15 minutes before carving.

Hazepeper

Peppered hare

6 servings

1 (4 pound) hare or substitute
   chicken
1 cup red wine
½ cup red wine vinegar
1 carrot, peeled and sliced
1 onion, finely chopped
3 juniper berries
1 bay leaf
4 peppercorns, crushed
   Salt
   Freshly ground black pepper
3 tablespoons butter
½ medium sized onion,
   finely chopped
½ cup thinly sliced fresh
   mushrooms
¼ cup chopped smoked ham
2 cups water
5 tablespoons flour
3 to 4 tablespoons butter,
   softened
2 tablespoons finely chopped
   parsley
1 cup crisp croutons

Cut the hare into serving
pieces and place in a bowl with
the wine, vinegar, carrot, onion,
juniper berries, bay leaf and
peppercorns. Cover the bowl
with plastic wrap and let the
hare marinate in the refrigerator
for 1 to 2 days. Remove the hare.
Strain and reserve the marinade.
Wipe the pieces of hare
thoroughly dry and rub them
with salt and pepper. Heat the
butter in a casserole and quickly
brown the hare on all sides over
high heat. Remove the hare
from the pan. Add the onion,
mushrooms and ham and sauté
for about 5 minutes. Remove
from the pan and set aside.
Pour off all the fat from the pan.
Return the pieces of hare to the
pan along with the reserved
marinade and the water. Bring
to a simmer and cover the pan.
Cook over low heat for 1¼
hours. Return the onion,
mushrooms and ham to the pan
and simmer 15 minutes more.
Blend the flour and butter
together in a small bowl. Add
the mixture bit by bit to the
simmering liquid, stirring until
the sauce is thickened and
smooth. Arrange the meat on a
platter and pour the sauce over.
Garnish with parsley and
croutons. Serve with potatoes
and applesauce or red cabbage.

Hazebout met pruimen

Hare with prunes

4 servings

- 3 tablespoons butter
- 2 hare legs or substitute turkey legs
- 1 onion, finely chopped
- 3 tablespoons flour
- 1½ cups red wine
- ½ teaspoon salt
  Freshly ground black pepper
- 2 teaspoons vinegar
- 1 tablespoon sugar
- 1 cup dried pitted prunes

Melt the butter and sauté the hare legs over moderately high heat until nicely browned. Remove from the pan, add onion and sauté in the same butter until tender. Sprinkle on the flour and cook, stirring, for 1 minute. Add the red wine gradually, stirring to scrape up the brown bits clinging to the bottom of the pan. Return the hare legs to the pan and add salt, pepper, vinegar and sugar. Cover and simmer over low heat for 40 minutes. Add the prunes and continue cooking 30 minutes or until the hare legs are tender.

Brabants konijn

Rabbit Brabant style

4 servings

- 1 young (2½ to 3 pound) rabbit, cut into serving pieces or use chicken
- 1 medium sized onion, thinly sliced
- 1 teaspoon thyme
- 1 bay leaf
- 1 cup red wine vinegar
- ½ cup water
- ¼ teaspoon salt
  Freshly ground black pepper
- ½ cup flour
- 2 tablespoons butter
- ½ pound prunes, soaked overnight in water.
- 1 tablespoon brown sugar
- ½ cup beer
- 2 tablespoons flour

Place the rabbit pieces in a shallow pan. Combine the onion, thyme, bay leaf, vinegar and water and pour the mixture over the rabbit. Cover the pan tightly with plastic wrap or aluminum foil and allow the rabbit to marinate overnight in the refrigerator. Remove the rabbit from the marinade and dry the pieces thoroughly. Sprinkle with salt and pepper and roll in flour. Heat the butter and brown the rabbit on all sides over high heat until golden. Strain and add the marinade. Lower the heat, cover the pan and simmer slowly for 30 minutes. Add the drained prunes and brown sugar and simmer 15 minutes more. Combine the beer and flour and stir until smooth. Add the beer mixture to the rabbit, stirring constantly until the sauce is thickened. Place the rabbit and prunes on a warm serving dish and pour the sauce over.

Vlaams konijn met mosterd

Rabbit with mustard

4 servings

- 1 young (2½–3 pound) rabbit or substitute chicken
- 4 tablespoons mild (Dijon type) mustard
- 1 teaspoon salt
  Freshly ground black pepper
- 6 thin slices bacon
- ½ cup heavy cream
- 1 tablespoon flour combined with
  2 tablespoons heavy cream

Spread 2 tablespoons of the mustard in the cavity of the rabbit. Sprinkle the outside with salt and pepper. Cover the rabbit with bacon slices and spread the bacon with the remaining mustard. Place the rabbit in a heavy casserole just large enough to hold it. Cover and cook in a 350° oven for 1 to 1½ hours or until tender. Transfer the rabbit to a heated platter. Add cream to the pan juices and bring to a simmer. Stir in the flour-cream mixture with a wire whisk and cook, stirring, 2 to 3 minutes. Cover the rabbit with a little of the sauce and pass the rest separately. This dish is equally good using chicken so don't hesitate to try it.

Vegetable dishes

Vlaamse asperges

Flemish asparagus

4 servings

3–4 pounds asparagus
  4 hard boiled eggs, halved
  8 thin slices boiled ham,
     formed into rolls
  1 cup melted butter
     Small dish of grated nutmeg

When Dutch school children come home and ask what is for dinner, the answer is not 'steak' or 'pork chops,' but 'cauliflower' or 'carrots.'
When the Dutch housewife plans her evening meal, she thinks first of the vegetables and then plans the rest of the meal around them. In Holland, the vegetables are more important than the meat, and the Dutch have always prided themselves on their preparation. The oldest street in Amsterdam is called 'Warmoesstraat,' the street of the vegetables, because in the Middle Ages vegetable growers lived there. If we read the bills and accounts of ancient students' dormitories, hospitals and old people's homes, we find that large amounts were spent on vegetables: carrots, onions, turnips, cabbages, spinach, leeks and beans. In the cookbooks used in the homes of rich Amsterdam merchants in the 18th century, there are refined recipes for such luxury vegetables as artichokes and asparagus.
Today, many Dutch vegetables are cultivated in greenhouses so that fresh fall vegetables can be had at Christmas. It might be no great hardship to do without meat on the table for one day, but for the Dutch not a day can go by without fresh vegetables.

Wash the asparagus, break off the woody part of the stalks and peel the lower third of asparagus spears. Tie the asparagus in bunches of 8 to 10 spears. Drop the asparagus into boiling, salted water to cover and cook 10 to 15 minutes or until the stalks are just tender. Do not allow the asparagus to become limp and soggy. Drain the asparagus, untie the bundles and place on a warm serving dish with the tips all pointing in the same direction. Garnish with the eggs and ham. Serve the melted butter and nutmeg separately. Traditionally, each diner is given a small bowl in which he flakes the egg with a fork and adds melted butter and nutmeg. He then dips the asparagus spears into the prepared sauce before eating. This dish is served as a main course.

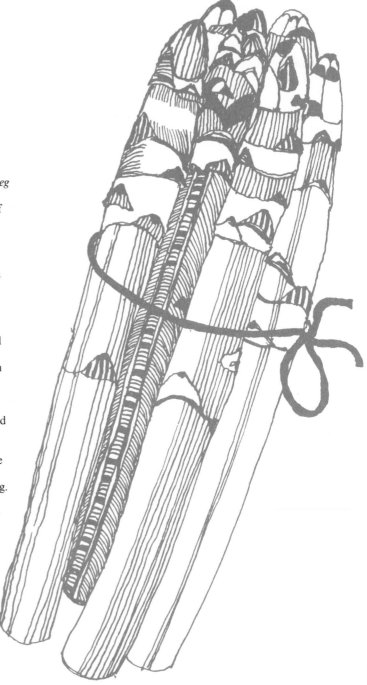

Gevulde slakropjes

Stuffed lettuce heads

4 servings

- 4 small heads Boston or Bibb lettuce
- 4 hard boiled eggs
- ½ pound ham or bacon, thinly sliced
- 2 tablespoons butter
- ½ cup bouillon

Bring plenty of salted water to a boil. Add the lettuce, blanch for 2 minutes and drain. Peel the eggs and stuff each lettuce head with an egg. Wrap the thinly sliced ham or bacon around the lettuce heads and tie. Melt butter in an ovenproof dish and coat the lettuce with the melted butter. Arrange the lettuce heads in the dish, pour over bouillon and heat 5 to 10 minutes in a preheated 350° oven. Serve with fried or mashed potatoes.

Selderij sla

Celery salad

4 servings

- 1 bunch celery
  Mayonnaise

Wash the celery and cut the stalks into match-like strips. Drop the celery into boiling, salted water and cook 3 minutes. Immediately drain and rinse the celery under cold, running water until the celery is cool. Chill for 1 hour. Serve the celery dressed with mayonnaise.

Naakte kindertjes in het gras

Naked children in the grass

4 servings

- 1 pound dried lima beans
- 4 cups water
- 2 teaspoons salt
- 1½ pounds green beans
- 4 tablespoons butter
- 1 tablespoon sugar

Soak the beans overnight in the salted water. Bring the beans to a boil and cook for 45 minutes. Cut the green beans into 1 inch pieces. Add to the lima beans and simmer over low heat for another 15 minutes. Drain, transfer to a warm serving dish and stir in the butter and sugar.

Gevulde uien

Stuffed onions

6 servings

- 6 large onions
- 2 tablespoons butter
- ½ pound lean ground pork
- 2 tablespoons tomato purée
- ½ teaspoon salt
  Freshly ground black pepper
- 3 tablespoons grated Gouda or Parmesan cheese
- 1½ tablespoons butter
- 1 cup beef broth

Cut the tops off the onions and scoop out as much of the insides as possible, leaving a shell about ¼ inch thick. Cook the onions in boiling salted water for 5 minutes and turn upside down to drain. Chop the insides of the onion very finely and sauté in the 2 tablespoons butter over very low heat for 15 minutes. Combine the onions with the pork, tomato purée, salt and pepper. Stuff the onions with this mixture, top with grated cheese and dot with butter. Place the onions in a shallow buttered oven proof dish and add the broth. Bake the onions in a 400° oven for 30 minutes, basting occasionally with the broth.

Vlaamse rodekool

Flemish red cabbage

4 servings

- 1 red cabbage, shredded
- 2 tablespoons vinegar
- 1 tablespoon salt
- 2 tablespoons butter
- 1 medium sized onion, finely chopped
- 2 cooking apples, peeled, cored and chopped
- 1 tablespoon sugar
- 1 clove
- 1 bay leaf
- ¼ teaspoon thyme
  Freshly ground black pepper
- ½ cup water

Combine cabbage, vinegar and salt and let the mixture stand 30 minutes. Meanwhile, melt the butter and sauté the onion 2 minutes. Combine all the ingredients in a large saucepan and bring to a boil. Lower the heat, cover and simmer slowly 1 hour. Serve hot.

Kruidige rodekool

Spiced red cabbage

4 servings

- ¼ cup butter
- 1 cup water
- 1 teaspoon salt
- 1 small red cabbage, finely shredded
- 2 cooking apples, peeled, cored and sliced
- 3 cloves
- 1 tablespoon sugar
  Dash of vinegar

In a saucepan, place 1 tablespoon butter, the water and salt. Add red cabbage, apples and cloves and simmer 45 minutes. Add remaining butter, sugar and vinegar and simmer for another 5 minutes. Remove cloves before serving.

Gegratineerde bloemkool

Cauliflower from the oven

4 servings

- 1 cauliflower
- 3 tablespoons butter
- 3 tablespoons flour
- 3 cups milk
- ½ teaspoon salt
  Freshly ground black pepper
- 6 tablespoons grated Gouda or Parmesan cheese
- 2 tablespoons dry breadcrumbs

Wash and trim the cauliflower and cook in boiling salted water to cover for 15 to 20 minutes. In a saucepan, heat 2 tablespoons butter, stir in flour and gradually add milk, stirring constantly. Cook for 3 minutes. Season with salt and pepper. Remove from the heat and stir in 3 tablespoons grated cheese. Place the cauliflower in an oven proof dish and pour the sauce over. Sprinkle with remaining cheese and breadcrumbs and dot with remaining 1 tablespoon butter. Bake in a 350° oven for 15 minutes, or until golden brown.

Bloemkool met bessesap

Cauliflower with blackberry sauce

4 servings

- 1 head cauliflower
- ¾ cup water
- ½ cup blackberry or blueberry juice
- 1 tablespoon cornstarch

Discard the green leaves from the cauliflower and cook the whole cauliflower in boiling salted water for 15 to 20 minutes or until tender. Meanwhile, prepare the sauce. Bring the water to a boil. Combine the blackberry juice and cornstarch and add to the boiling water, stirring constantly until the sauce has thickened. Drain the cauliflower, place it on a serving dish and pour over the prepared sauce. Serve with fried potatoes.

Koolwarmoes

Cabbage and salt pork

4 servings

1 quart milk
1 pound salt pork, cubed
3 onions, chopped
1 white cabbage, shredded
½ teaspoon salt
Freshly ground black pepper
⅛ teaspoon nutmeg
2 tablespoons flour combined with
2 tablespoons cold milk

Bring milk and salt pork to a boil. Add onions, shredded cabbage, salt, pepper and nutmeg and cook gently for 20 minutes or until the vegetables are tender. Add the flour mixture to the cabbage, stirring constantly. Cook until slightly thickened.

Gebakken aardappelen met kaas

Potatoes with cheese

4 servings

6 tablespoons butter
2 pounds potatoes, peeled and thinly sliced
1 teaspoon salt
½ pound Gouda cheese, cut into small cubes

Heat the butter in a large skillet with sloping sides. Add the sliced potatoes and salt and cook, pressing down with the back of a spatula, until golden brown. Turn the potatoes and cook until brown on the other side. Add the cheese and cook until it melts. Serve piping hot.

Spruitjes met kaas

Brussels sprouts with cheese

4 servings

1 quart Brussels sprouts, washed and trimmed
1 cup beef broth
6 tablespoons grated Gouda or Edam cheese
Dash of nutmeg
2 tablespoons butter

Bring plenty of salted water to a boil and add the Brussels sprouts. Simmer 10 to 15 minutes or until tender. Drain. Arrange the sprouts in a buttered shallow ovenproof dish. Pour on beef broth and sprinkle with grated cheese and nutmeg. Dot with butter. Place in a preheated 350° oven for 5 to 7 minutes or until the cheese has melted.

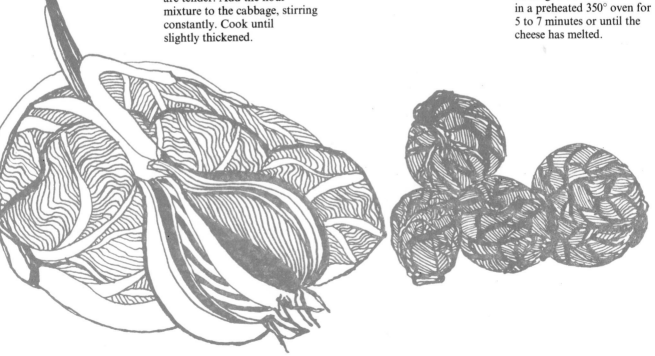

Brussels lof met ham

Gevuld witlof

Brabantse puree

Bietjes in speksaus

Endive with ham

4 servings (main course)

    8 endives
    8 thin slices boiled ham
 ½ cup beef broth
    3 cups mashed potatoes
 ½ teaspoon grated nutmeg
    2 tablespoons butter

Drop the endives into boiling salted water and simmer 8 to 10 minutes. Drain and wrap each endive in a slice of ham. Place them snugly in a shallow baking dish and add the broth. Spread the mashed potatoes over the endive so that they are completely covered. Dust with nutmeg and dot with butter. Bake in a 425° oven for 15 minutes.

Stuffed endive

4 servings

    4 endives
 ¼ pound ground veal
 ¼ pound ground pork
    1 egg, lightly beaten
    1 slice toasted bread
    1 tablespoon milk
    1 shallot or scallion,
        finely chopped
 ½ teaspoon salt
        Freshly ground black pepper
    4 tablespoons butter

Simmer the endives in boiling salted water for 5 minutes. Rinse under cold running water and drain. Combine the veal, pork and egg. Soak the bread in the milk, crumble and add to the meat mixture. Mix in the shallot, salt and pepper. Spread the leaves of the endive apart as much as possible and fill the center with the meat mixture. Press the leaves together and tie each endive tightly in 2 places with thread. Melt the butter in a skillet and sauté the endive slowly on all sides until very light brown. If the endive starts to brown too much or tends to stick to the pan, add water, 1 tablespoon at a time. Lower the heat, cover the pan and cook very slowly about 30 minutes. Remove the threads and serve.

Purée Brabant style

6 servings

    1 pound Brussels sprouts
    1 pound potatoes
    5 tablespoons butter
    1 onion, finely chopped
 ½ teaspoon salt
        Freshly ground black pepper
        Dash of nutmeg
    5 tablespoons milk

Drop the Brussels sprouts into plenty of boiling, salted water and cook 10 to 12 minutes or until tender. Peel the potatoes and cook, covered, in boiling, salted water about 20 minutes or until tender. Meanwhile, melt 2 tablespoons butter and sauté the onion until tender but do not allow it to brown. Drain the Brussels sprouts and potatoes and mash them together. Add the onion, remaining butter and all the other ingredients and combine thoroughly. Transfer to a warm serving dish and serve immediately.

Beets in bacon sauce

4 servings

    2 tablespoons butter
    1 onion, finely chopped
    1 cooking apple, peeled,
        cored and chopped
        Juice of 1 lemon
    3 cloves
    2 pounds cooked beets,
        grated or cubed

In a saucepan, melt the butter and add the onion, apple, lemon juice and cloves. Cook slowly for 15 minutes. Add the beets and simmer 10 minutes more.

For the sauce:
 ½ pound bacon, diced
    1 onion, chopped
    2 tablespoons flour
    2 cups water
    1 tablespoon vinegar
 ¼ teaspoon salt
        Freshly ground black pepper

Fry the bacon in a heavy saucepan until the fat is rendered. Pour off all but 2 tablespoons fat. Add onion and sauté in the bacon fat until soft. Stir in the flour and cook 2 minutes. Gradually add water and vinegar, stirring constantly until a smooth sauce is formed. Season with salt and pepper. Combine the sauce with the beets and serve hot.

Worteltjes en erwtjes

Carrots and peas

4 servings

 1 pound baby carrots, peeled
½ teaspoon salt
 1 tablespoon butter
 3 tablespoons cream
 3 cups hot cooked green peas
 1 tablespoon finely chopped
   parsley

Place the carrots in a saucepan, add salt and water to cover. Bring to a simmer, cover the pan and cook slowly for 20 to 30 minutes or until carrots are tender. Drain and add butter and cream. Toss until the carrots are coated and gleaming. Place the peas in the center of a serving dish and surround with the carrots. Sprinkle with parsley. Serve this dish with small boiled potatoes and a Dutch steak. (See page 46.)

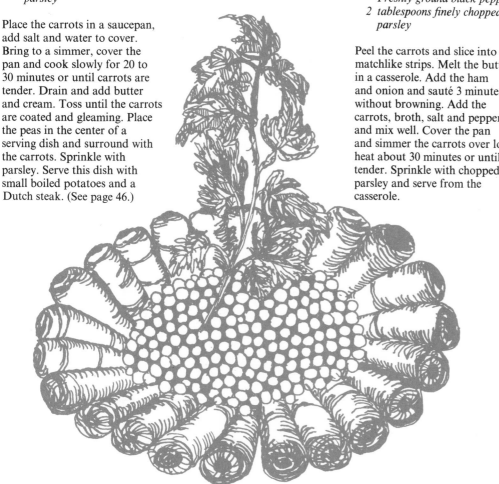

Vlaamse wortelen

Flemish carrots

4 to 6 servings

 2 pounds carrots
 3 tablespoons butter
¼ pound cooked ham, minced
 1 onion, finely chopped
½ cup beef broth
½ teaspoon salt
   Freshly ground black pepper
 2 tablespoons finely chopped
   parsley

Peel the carrots and slice into matchlike strips. Melt the butter in a casserole. Add the ham and onion and sauté 3 minutes without browning. Add the carrots, broth, salt and pepper and mix well. Cover the pan and simmer the carrots over low heat about 30 minutes or until tender. Sprinkle with chopped parsley and serve from the casserole.

Carottes à l'ardennaise

Carrots Ardennes style

4 servings

 1 pound carrots, peeled
¼ pound sliced bacon
 1 onion, finely chopped
 3 tablespoons flour
 1 cup hot water
¼ teaspoon salt
   Freshly ground black pepper
   Dash of nutmeg
 2 tablespoons sugar
 2 tablespoons finely chopped
   parsley

Cut the carrots into very thin strips and dice the bacon. Fry the bacon in a heavy casserole until the fat is rendered. Add the onion and sauté in the bacon fat a few minutes. Sprinkle in the flour and cook 1 minute. Gradually add the water, stirring constantly until a thick sauce forms. Add the carrot strips, salt, pepper, nutmeg and sugar. Cover the pan and simmer over very low heat until the carrots are tender. Sprinkle with freshly chopped parsley.

Desserts

Riz gratiné liégeoise

Rice au gratin Liège style

6 servings

For the rice:
- 4 cups milk
- 1 cup rice
- ¼ teaspoon salt
- ¾ cup sugar
- 1 teaspoon vanilla

For the applesauce:
- 1½ pounds cooking apples
- ½ cup sugar
- ½ cup raisins, soaked in hot water until plump and drained
- 1 teaspoon cinnamon
- 3 tablespoons water
- ½ cup freshly made breadcrumbs
- 2 tablespoons butter

Place the milk, rice, salt and sugar in a saucepan and bring to a boil, stirring constantly. Lower the heat, cover the pan and simmer slowly for 25 minutes or until rice is tender and the mixture resembles thick soup. Meanwhile, peel, core and chop the apples. Place them in a heavy pan with the sugar, raisins, cinnamon and water. Cook over very low heat until the apples are soft. Force the mixture through a sieve to form applesauce. When the rice is tender, stir in the vanilla and place half of the rice in a lightly buttered casserole. Cover with the applesauce and then the remaining rice. Sprinkle the rice with breadcrumbs and dot with butter. Place the casserole under a preheated broiler for a few minutes until the breadcrumbs are golden brown. Serve warm, or chill in the refrigerator and serve cold.

Repje den brij

Rice with currants and apples

8 servings

- 3 cups sweet white wine
- 2 cups rice
- 1 cup currants
- 12 cooking apples, peeled, cored and sliced
  Butter
  Bowl of sugar
  Dish of cinnamon

Place the wine, rice, currants and apples in a saucepan and bring to a boil, stirring constantly. Lower the heat, cover and cook slowly about 25 minutes or until rice is tender. Transfer to a glass bowl and serve. Pass butter, sugar and cinnamon so that each diner may serve himself to taste. In Holland, this dish is served as a complete meal.

Rijst met krenten en rozijnen

Rice with currants and raisins

6 to 8 servings

- 3¾ cups water
- 1½ cups rice
- 1 cup white raisins
- ½ cup currants
- 1 strip lemon rind
  Butter
  Sugar
  Cinnamon

Bring the water to a boil. Add the rice, raisins, currants and lemon rind and stir once with a fork. Lower the heat, cover the pan and cook over low heat 20 to 30 minutes or until all the liquid has been absorbed by the rice. Place in a warm serving dish. Pass butter, sugar and cinnamon separately in small dishes, so each person can flavor the rice according to his own taste.

Begijnerijst

Baguine rice

4 servings

- ½ cup rice
- 2 cups milk
- ¼ teaspoon salt
- 1 cinnamon stick
- ½ cup powdered sugar
- ⅛ teaspoon saffron threads
  Brown sugar

Place the rice in a pan with the milk, salt, cinnamon stick, powdered sugar and saffron and bring to a boil, stirring constantly. Lower the heat, cover and simmer very slowly for about 45 minutes. Place the rice in individual serving dishes, cool completely and sprinkle with brown sugar.

Griesmeelpudding met bessesap

Farina pudding with red currant sauce

4 servings

For the pudding:
- 4 cups milk
- ⅔ cup farina
- 2 tablespoons cornstarch
- 4 tablespoons sugar
- 1 tablespoon butter
- 1 teaspoon vanilla
- 1 egg, separated

For the sauce:
- 1½ cups red currant juice or black currant juice
- ¾ cup water
- 1 cinnamon stick
  Rind of 1 lemon, cut into strips
- 2½ tablespoons cornstarch dissolved in 3 tablespoons water
- 6 tablespoons sugar

Bring the milk to a boil. Combine the farina, cornstarch and sugar and gradually add this mixture to the boiling milk, stirring constantly. Continue stirring and cook 10 minutes or until thickened. Remove from the heat and beat in the butter, vanilla and egg yolk. Beat the egg white until stiff and gently fold it into the pudding. Rinse a pudding mold with cold water and pour in the pudding. Chill until set. To prepare the sauce: place the juice, water, cinnamon stick and lemon rind in a saucepan and bring to a boil. Cook gently for 3 minutes, then stir in the cornstarch mixture. Cook 2 minutes and add the sugar to the sauce. Remove and discard the lemon rind and cinnamon stick. Unmold pudding on a platter and pour the warm sauce over.

Gruau aux prunes

Prune porridge

6 servings

- 1 pound prunes, soaked in cold water overnight
- ¾ cup sugar
- ½ cup water
- 1 tablespoon cornstarch dissolved in 1 tablespoon water
- 1 quart milk
- ¼ teaspoon salt
- ½ cup sugar
- 5 tablespoons semolina
- 2 egg yolks

Drain prunes, cut them in half and remove the pits. Place them in a pan with ¾ cup sugar and water. Put the pan over very low heat until the liquid comes to a boil. Drain the prunes and reserve the liquid. Bring the liquid to a simmer and thicken it slightly with the cornstarch mixture. Set aside to cool. Bring all but ½ cup of the milk to a boil and add the salt and sugar. Combine the semolina with the remaining cold milk and stir until smooth. Gradually add the semolina mixture to the boiling milk, stirring constantly with a wire whisk. Remove the pan from the heat, cool the mixture a few minutes and beat in the egg yolks. Transfer to a glass serving dish and chill. When ready to serve, place the prunes on top of the semolina and pour over the thickened prune liquid.

Turfjes met bessesap

"Bread" with red currant sauce

4 servings

- 4 *thick slices of white bread, crusts removed*
- 6 *tablespoons butter*

For the sauce:
- 1½ *cups red currant juice or black currant juice*
- ¾ *cup water*
- 1 *cinnamon stick Rind of 1 lemon, cut into strips*
- 2½ *tablespoons cornstarch dissolved in 3 tablespoons water*
- 6 *tablespoons sugar*

Cut the slices of bread into strips, 3 × ½ × 1½ inches. Heat butter in a skillet and sauté the bread strips on all sides until golden brown. Arrange them on a dish and pour the warm red currant sauce over.

To make the sauce:
Place the red currant juice, water, cinnamon stick, and lemon rind in a saucepan and bring to a boil. Cook gently for 3 minutes. Stir in the cornstarch mixture to thicken. Cool 2 minutes and add the sugar to the sauce. Remove the cinnamon stick and lemon rind. Keep the sauce warm.

Watergruwel

Barley with red currant juice

6 to 8 servings

- 4 *cups water*
- ½ *cup barley, washed*
- 1 *cinnamon stick*
- 2 *cups red currant, blackberry or raspberry juice (or substitute other fruit juice) Juice of 1 lemon*
- ½ *cup sugar*
- 1 *cup raisins*

Bring the water to a boil and add the barley and cinnamon stick. Lower the heat and simmer very slowly, uncovered, for 1½ hours. Add the remaining ingredients and bring to a boil. Lower the heat and continue simmering slowly for ½ hour or until the mixture is the consistency of thick soup. Remove the cinnamon stick. Serve hot or cold.

La Truleye

Beer porridge

4 servings

- 4 *cups beer*
- 2 *cups finely crumbled spice cake*
- ½ *cup brown sugar*
- 1 *teaspoon cinnamon Dash of nutmeg*
- 1 *egg, lightly beaten*
- 4 *teaspoons butter, melted*

Place the beer, cake, sugar, cinnamon and nutmeg in a saucepan. Bring to a simmer and cook over very low heat, stirring constantly. Remove the pan from the heat and let the mixture cool 5 minutes. Stir in the egg and butter and serve immediately.

Chocoladevla met mandarijntjes

Chocolate custard with mandarin oranges

6 servings

- 1 *egg*
- 1 *egg yolk*
- 4 *tablespoons sugar*
- 3 *tablespoons powdered Dutch cocoa*
- 3 *tablespoons cornstarch*
- 3 *cups milk*
- 1 *small can Mandarin oranges*

Beat together the egg and egg yolk until frothy. Add the sugar and beat until the mixture is thickened. Beat in the cocoa, cornstarch and ¼ cup of the milk. Heat the remaining milk until simmering and add to the egg mixture, stirring constantly. Transfer to a saucepan and cook over low heat, stirring constantly until the custard is thickened. Pour into individual serving dishes and chill until firm. Decorate with Mandarin oranges and serve.

Chocolate custard with mandarin oranges (recipe page 68, 4th column)

Gort met abrikozen en rozijnen

Barley with apricots and raisins

4 to 6 servings

   1 cup dried apricots
   6 cups water
   1 cup barley, washed
       Rind of ½ lemon, cut into
       thin strips
   ½ cup raisins
   ¼ cup sugar
   1 tablespoon cornstarch
       dissolved in
       1½ tablespoons cold water

Soak the apricots overnight in water to cover. Bring the 6 cups water to a boil and add the barley and lemon rind. Cook over medium heat for 45 minutes to 1 hour. Drain, remove the lemon rind and pack the barley into an oiled 4 cup ring mold. Refrigerate until firm. In the meantime, bring the apricots to a simmer in their soaking water. Add the raisins and cook over low heat 10 minutes. Stir in the sugar and enough of the cornstarch mixture to form a thick sauce. Chill the apricot mixture. When ready to serve, unmold the barley on a flat serving dish. Fill the center with the apricot mixture and serve.

Eiers en beiers

Eggs and cherries

4 servings

 1 *pound cherries, pitted, or*
 1 *(1 pound) can pitted Bing*
   cherries, drained
 4 *eggs*
½ *cup sugar*
 1 *teaspoon cinnamon*

For fresh cherries, barely cover them with water, bring to a boil and cook 5 minutes. (Canned cherries need not be cooked.) Drain the cherries, purée in a blender and force through a sieve. In the bowl of an electric mixer, beat the eggs until foamy. Add the sugar and cinnamon and continue beating until thick and creamy. Fold in the cherry purée. Chill thoroughly and serve in a glass bowl.

Pruimenkreuze

Plum soup

4 to 6 servings

 ½ *pound dried plums or prunes*
1½ *cups golden raisins*
  6 *cups water*
  2 *tablespoons molasses*
  2 *tablespoons butter*
  ¼ *teaspoon vinegar*
  1 *tablespoon cornstarch*
    dissolved in
    1 *tablespoon water*

Soak plums or prunes and raisins overnight in the water. Bring to a boil, add molasses, butter and vinegar and cook 5 minutes. Stir the dissolved cornstarch into the soup to thicken. Serve hot.

Haagse bluf

The Hague bluff

6 to 8 servings

 3 *egg whites*
 ⅛ *teaspoon cream of tartar*
 6 *tablespoons sugar*
1¼ *cups red currant juice,*
   raspberry juice or substitute
   other fruit juice

In the bowl of an electric mixer, beat the egg whites with the cream of tartar until foamy. Add sugar gradually and beat until stiff. Add the fruit juice a few drops at a time, beating constantly. Serve immediately with sugar wafers.

Hangop

Hang up

6 to 8 servings

 2 *quarts buttermilk*
½–¾ *cup sugar*
6–8 *Dutch rusks, crumbled*
    Cinnamon

Place 2 wet linen tea towels in a colander. Set the colander over a pan or in the sink and pour the buttermilk into the colander. Let the buttermilk drip through the double thickness of linen for 3 to 4 hours or until as thick as cream. From time to time scrape the thickened part of the buttermilk into a bowl. When all the thickened buttermilk has been transferred to the bowl, beat in the sugar with an electric mixer. Beat until completely smooth. Chill several hours. Serve in individual bowls and sprinkle with the rusks and cinnamon. **Note:** The watery part of the buttermilk will drip through the towels while the solid part has the appearance of soft cottage cheese.

Poires Bayard

Pears Bayard

6 servings

4 cups milk
2 tablespoons semolina
¾ cup sugar
2 eggs, separated
6 ripe pears
1 lemon, cut in half
2 cups water
2 cups sugar
1 cinnamon stick
1 teaspoon vanilla
⅓ cup toasted slivered almonds

Bring all but ¼ cup milk to a boil. Combine the semolina with the reserved ¼ cup cold milk. Stir the semolina mixture and sugar into the boiling milk with a wire whisk and cook, stirring, until slightly thickened. Remove the pan from the heat. Add the egg yolks to the milk mixture, beating them in with a wire whisk. Beat the egg whites until stiff. Fold the egg whites in until thoroughly incorporated Transfer the custard to a buttered casserole, cover and bake in a 400° oven for 15 minutes. Cool, then refrigerate the custard. Peel the pears, cut them in half and remove the cores. Squeeze lemon juice over the pears to prevent them from darkening. In a saucepan, place the water, sugar, cinnamon stick and vanilla and bring to a boil. Lower the heat, add the pears and simmer 3 minutes. Remove the pears from the syrup and chill them. Serve the pears on top of the custard and sprinkle with toasted almonds.

Poires cuites

Baked pears

6 servings

1½ cups brown sugar
1 cup water
1 teaspoon cinnamon
6 firm, ripe pears

Combine the sugar, water and cinnamon in a saucepan. Bring to a boil and cook until the sugar is completely dissolved and the syrup is thickened. Place the pears upright in a casserole and pour the syrup over them. See that as much of the syrup as possible clings to the pears. Bake the pears in a 350° oven 30 to 40 minutes or until tender. Serve warm or cold.

Salade à l'encre

Inky salad

4 servings

1 box fresh blueberries
½ cup sugar
1 cup dry red wine

Wash and pick over the blueberries. Drain and place them in a glass bowl. Add the sugar and wine and mix gently with a wooden spoon. Refrigerate for 2 hours before serving.

Fraises au fromage rose

Strawberries and cottage cheese

6 to 8 servings

3 pints strawberries
2 tablespoons Kirsch
5 tablespoons powdered sugar
1 (8 ounce) carton creamed cottage cheese
1 egg yolk

Wash the strawberries and remove the stems. Sprinkle half the strawberries with the Kirsch and half of the sugar. Force the remaining strawberries through a sieve. In the bowl of an electric mixer, beat the cottage cheese with the egg yolk and remaining sugar until the mixture is smooth. Fold in the strawberry purée. Place the cottage cheese mixture in a glass dish and arrange the whole strawberries on top. Serve slightly chilled.

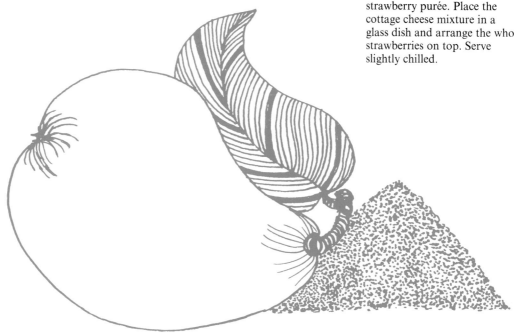

Kersepap

Cherry soup

10 servings

    1 *pound fresh cherries*
    2 *cups flour*
   10 *cups milk*
    1 *teaspoon cinnamon*
    1 *cup sugar*

Place the cherries in a saucepan
and barely cover with water.
Bring to a simmer and cook
5 minutes. Drain and force
cherries through a sieve. Stir the
flour into 4 cups cold milk to
make a smooth paste. Slowly
add the flour mixture to the
remaining milk stirring
constantly. Add the cinnamon,
sugar and cherry purée. Bring
to a boil and cook, stirring
constantly, for 5 minutes.

Appelepap

Apple soup

10 servings

    1 *pound cooking apples,*
       cored and quartered
   ¼ *cup water*
    2 *cups flour*
   10 *cups buttermilk*
    1 *teaspoon ground anise*
    6 *tablespoons molasses*

Place the apples in a heavy
saucepan and add the water.
Cover and cook over low heat
until the apples are soft enough
to mash. Check from time to
time to see if the apples are
sticking. If so, add water,
1 tablespoon at a time to
prevent sticking. Stir the flour
into 4 cups cold milk to make a
smooth paste. Mash the apples
in the saucepan and add the
remaining milk to the apples.
Gradually add the flour mixture
stirring constantly. Continue
stirring and bring to a boil.
Add the anise and molasses
and serve immediately.

Rabarberpudding

Rhubarb pudding

4 servings

  1 *pound rhubarb*
  3 *cups water*
  2 *cups sugar*
  1 *strip lemon peel*
  2 *packages unflavored gelatin*
½ *cup white wine*

Cut the rhubarb into 1 inch pieces and poach 20 to 25 minutes in the water with the sugar and lemon peel. Remove lemon peel and strain. Reserve the rhubarb. Dissolve gelatin in the liquid. Cool 2 minutes, then add the white wine and rhubarb. Chill until set. Serve cold. Decorate with whipped cream.

Jan in de zak

John in the sack

1 package dry yeast
¼ cup lukewarm water
3 cups sifted all purpose flour
1 teaspoon salt
1 egg, lightly beaten
¾ cup lukewarm milk
⅓ cup currants
⅓ cup raisins
¼ cup chopped candied peel

Sprinkle the yeast over the water and stir to dissolve. Place flour and salt in a bowl. Add beaten egg and lukewarm milk and blend well. Add currants, raisins and candied peel and mix thoroughly. Finally, add the yeast mixture and blend well. Place the dough in an oiled bowl, cover and let rise in a warm place for 45 minutes. Meanwhile, sprinkle a clean wet cloth or pillow case with flour. Roll the dough into an oblong shape and tie loosely in the cloth, leaving room for expansion of the dough. Tie the ends firmly and stick a large safety pin in the center. Place the dough in a steamer and steam 2 to 3 hours over boiling water. Remove from the cloth and serve hot with melted butter and brown sugar. Do not cut the bread with a knife, but use a thin string.

Wentelteefjes

Turn-overs

4 servings

1 teaspoon ground cinnamon
2 tablespoons sugar
1 egg, lightly beaten
1 cup lukewarm milk
* Pinch of salt*
8 slices day-old bread, crusts removed
3 tablespoons butter

Combine cinnamon and sugar. Add the egg, milk and salt. Soak the slices of bread in this mixture. Heat the butter in a skillet and fry the bread slices slowly on both sides. Serve hot, sprinkled with sugar and cinnamon.

Zaans brood

Bread from the Zaan area

6 servings

1½ cups milk
12 slices day-old bread, crusts removed
* Pinch of salt*
¼ cup sugar
1 egg, lightly beaten
1 teaspoon vanilla
3 tablespoons butter
½ cup raisins
* Powdered sugar*

Bring the milk to a boil. Crumble the bread and add it to the milk. Stir constantly until a thick porridge is formed. Cool the mixture to lukewarm. Add the salt, sugar, egg, vanilla, butter and raisins and mix well. Butter an 8 inch spring form or other cake tin and pour in the mixture. Bake in a preheated 350° oven for 35 minutes. Let cool 5 minutes before removing from the pan. Serve covered with a thick layer of powdered sugar.

Drie in de pan

Three in a pan

4 servings

2 cups self-rising flour
¼ teaspoon salt
1 egg
1½ cups lukewarm milk
1 cup mixed currants and raisins
1 tablespoon butter or oil
* Powdered sugar*

Combine the flour and salt in a bowl. Make a well in the center. Drop in the egg and pour in 1 cup lukewarm milk. Blend well into a smooth batter. Add the remaining milk and the currants and raisins. Heat the butter or oil in a heavy frying pan until very hot. Pour batter for 3 pancakes into the hot fat and fry them, 3 at a time, on both sides until golden brown. Serve hot with powdered sugar and a dot of butter on top of each.

Staphorster fleeren

Waffles from Staphorst

4 servings

    1 cup rye flour
    1 cup white flour
    ¼ cup brown sugar
    ½ teaspoon powdered anise
    ½ cup (1 stick) melted butter
    ½ cup molasses
    4 eggs, lightly beaten
    1 cup water

Combine the rye and white flour, brown sugar and anise. In a large bowl, mix the butter molasses, eggs and water. Add the flour mixture and stir with a wire whisk until thoroughly combined. Bake the waffles in a hot waffle iron for about 7 minutes or until brown. They will be soft rather than crisp. If not eaten immediately, they may be stored in a tightly closed container and reheated in a 250° oven for about 5 minutes.

Spekpannekoekjes

Bacon pancakes

4 to 6 servings

    2 cups pancake mix
    2 eggs, lightly beaten
    2 cups milk
    2 tablespoons melted butter
    ½ pound sliced bacon
    1 tablespoon bacon fat
      Molasses or brown sugar

In a bowl, combine the pancake mix, eggs, milk and butter. Mix just until combined. Fry the bacon until crisp and drain on paper towels. Divide it into 4 or 6 portions. Heat the bacon fat very hot in a crêpe pan or skillet about the size of a dinner plate. Place 1 portion of the bacon in the pan and pour in a layer of pancake batter. Cook until holes appear on the surface of the pancake. Turn to brown the other side. Keep the pancakes warm in a 200° oven until all are cooked. Serve with molasses or brown sugar.

Kaaspannekoekjes

Cheese pancakes

4 servings

    1¼ cups pancake mix
     ¼ teaspoon salt
      3 eggs
    1½ cups milk
      1 tablespoon melted butter
      8 slices Gouda or Edam cheese
      1 cup chopped walnuts

Place the pancake mix and salt in a mixing bowl. Beat the eggs with the milk and stir in the butter. Add the liquid ingredients to the pancake mix and stir just until the mixture is well combined. Heat an oiled crêpe pan or other small frying pan until very hot. Make very thin pancakes and stack on a clean tea towel as they are done. You will need 12 pancakes for this recipe. The remaining pancakes may be wrapped in foil and frozen for future use. Place 4 pancakes on a buttered cookie sheet. Place a slice of cheese on top of each. Place another pancake, then a slice of cheese on top of each stack and end with a pancake. Place the cookie sheet in a preheated 275° oven for 15 minutes. Place each stack of pancakes on an individual serving dish and sprinkle the walnuts on top. Serve immediately.

SIDEUS RRONOBISQUISCONTRA NOS 1733

Pancakes have always been a great attraction for Dutch children and in many families there is a tradition that on rainy days during the vacation (and there are many rainy days in Holland) the children get to make their own pancakes.

Yogurt pancakes

Cheese pancakes (recipe page 75, 4th column)

Flensjes met yoghurt

Yogurt pancakes

4 servings

- 2 cups pancake mix
- 2 cups chicken broth
- 3 eggs
- ¼ teaspoon salt
  Freshly ground black pepper
- 1 tablespoon oil

For the filling:
- 1 tablespoon butter
- 1 small onion, finely chopped
- 2 cups plain yogurt
- 2 tablespoons finely chopped parsley
- 1 tablespoon finely chopped celery leaves
- ½ cup grated Gouda or Edam cheese
- 1 tablespoon tomato purée

In a bowl, blend together the pancake mix, broth, eggs, salt, pepper and oil. Cover the batter and set aside for 30 minutes. Meanwhile, prepare the filling. Heat the butter and sauté the onion until soft. Drain and combine with all the remaining ingredients. Stir the pancake batter again and cook the pancakes in an oiled crêpe pan or skillet until all the batter is used. Spread each pancake with some of the filling mixture and roll up into a cigarette shape. Arrange the rolls in a shallow buttered ovenproof dish and place in a preheated 350° oven for 10 to 15 minutes or until they are hot. Serve immediately.

Probably the first Dutch words that a foreigner learns are 'kopje koffie,' a cup of coffee. And it is very appropriate that the Dutchman calls his cup of coffee a 'mug of comfort.' Without coffee, life in Holland would be unthinkable. In offices, hospitals and factories, half the morning is spent looking forward to a cup of coffee, universally brought around at half past ten. The first thing that any host says to a visitor is 'Would you like a cup of coffee?' And even on trains (though the distances in Holland are short) coffee is almost always served. Dutch coffee is quite strong, but it is accompanied by a quantity of warm milk, and for a special treat, it is served with cream or whipped cream.
Cake always goes with coffee. Usually simple cakes and cookies are served, but for guests there are buttercakes or slices of ginger cake spread with butter. And for special occasions, such as birthdays (nowhere in the world celebrated more elaborately), there is often a pie, offered to everyone at the office, shop or factory. There are thousands of kinds of cakes for birthdays: with fruit, chocolate, and above all, whipped cream.

Pastry

Rozijnencake

Raisin cake

  10 *tablespoons butter*
  ¾ *cup sugar*
      Grated rind of 1 lemon
   3 *eggs*
   2 *cups flour*
   1 *teaspoon baking powder*
  ¼ *teaspoon salt*
  ¾ *cup raisins*
      Powdered sugar

In a bowl, cream the butter until soft. Add the sugar and beat until the mixture is light and fluffy. Beat in the lemon rind and add the eggs 1 at a time, beating well after each addition. Sift together the flour, baking powder and salt and add to the butter-egg mixture. Mix lightly and fold in the raisins. Spoon the batter into a buttered and floured loaf tin. Bake the cake in a preheated 300° oven for 1 to 1¼ hours or until the cake tests done. Let it cool in the pan for 5 minutes then turn out of the pan to cool further on a wire rack. Sprinkle the top with powdered sugar.

Speculaas

Spicy cakes

   3 *cups flour*
  ⅔ *cup butter, softened*
  ½ *cup brown sugar*
   1 *teaspoon baking powder*
  ¼ *teaspoon salt*
   2 *tablespoons milk*
   1 *teaspoon cinnamon*
  ½ *teaspoon nutmeg*
  ¼ *teaspoon ground cloves*
  ½ *cup slivered almonds*

Knead all the ingredients together into a soft ball, reserving a few almonds for decoration. Roll out on a floured board to a sheet ¼ inch thick and cut various shapes with cookie cutters or form gingerbread men. Butter a baking sheet and bake the cakes in a preheated 350° oven for 20 to 25 minutes or until brown. Cool on wire racks and decorate with the remaining almonds.

Kramiek

Raisin bread

2 loaves

   2 *packages dry yeast*
1¾ *cups lukewarm milk*
  ¼ *cup sugar*
   2 *teaspoons salt*
   3 *tablespoons melted butter*
4½ *to 5 cups all purpose flour*
1½ *cups raisins*

Sprinkle the yeast over the lukewarm milk and stir to dissolve. Stir in the sugar, salt and butter. Add the flour, ½ cup at a time, until the dough begins to pull away from the sides of the bowl. Turn the dough out onto a floured board and knead in as much more flour as necessary to prevent the dough from sticking to the board and your hands. Knead the dough until it is smooth and elastic. Shape the dough into a ball and place it in an oiled bowl. Cover with a damp cloth and let rise in a warm spot about 1 hour or until doubled in bulk. Punch the dough down and knead in the raisins. Return the dough to the bowl, cover and let rise another hour. Punch the dough down and divide into 2 equal pieces. Form each piece into a round loaf and place the loaves on an oiled baking sheet. Cover and let rise about 20 minutes. Bake in a preheated 425° oven for 30 minutes. Cool the loaves before slicing. Serve with sweet butter and coffee.

Dumkes

Small thumbs

2½ cups sifted all purpose flour
1½ cups sugar
⅓ cup finely chopped hazelnuts
  (filbert nuts)
1 teaspoon cinnamon
1 teaspoon powdered anise
3 eggs, lightly beaten

In a bowl, combine the flour, sugar, hazelnuts, cinnamon and anise. Add the beaten eggs and mix until all the ingredients are thoroughly blended. Pinch off pieces of dough and form cookies the shape of your thumb. Place on a buttered cookie sheet and bake in a preheated 375° oven for 20 to 25 minutes or until golden brown. Cool the cookies on wire racks. In the Dutch province of Friesland, "dumkes" are served with tea.

Appelbollen

Apple balls

8 servings

2 cups sifted all purpose flour
½ teaspoon salt
10 tablespoons butter
4 to 5 tablespoons cold water
8 sweet apples, peeled and cored
2 tablespoons sugar
2 teaspoons cinnamon
¼ cup raisins
2 tablespoons butter
1 egg, lightly beaten

Combine the flour and salt in a bowl. Cut the butter into the flour with a pastry blender or 2 knives until the mixture resembles coarse meal. Stir the water in with a fork. Add only as much as is necessary to make the dough stick together. Wrap the dough in waxed paper and refrigerate for 1 hour. Roll the dough into a rectangle on a floured board. Cut into 8 squares each large enough to enclose an apple. Center an apple on each square of pastry. Combine the sugar, cinnamon and raisins and stuff each apple with a little of the mixture. Dot the top with butter and gather the pastry up around the apple. Pinch the edges together to seal. Brush each apple ball with beaten egg. Place on a buttered baking sheet and bake in a preheated 375° oven for 25 minutes or until golden brown.

Weesper moppen

Almond cookies

40 to 45 cookies

1½ cups finely ground almonds
1¼ cups sugar
2 eggs
  Grated rind of 1 lemon

In a bowl, blend all the ingredients together thoroughly. Chill the dough in the refrigerator for about 2 hours. Shape the dough into a cylinder 1½ inches in diameter and cut into ¼ inch thick slices. Butter a cookie tin and cover with baking paper. Butter the paper very generously. Place the cookies well apart on the baking paper. Let them stand 1 hour so the dough will dry out a little. Bake the cookies in a preheated 350° oven for 20 minutes or until golden brown. Carefully remove them from the baking paper and cool on wire racks.

Limburgse vlaai

Pie from Limburg

1 package dry yeast
½ cup lukewarm milk
2½ cups flour
¼ teaspoon salt
3 tablespoons melted butter
1 egg, lightly beaten
¼ cup sugar

Sprinkle the yeast over the lukewarm milk and stir to dissolve. Combine the flour and salt in a bowl and make a well in the center. Add the yeast mixture, melted butter, egg and sugar and knead into a smooth and elastic dough. Place the dough in an oiled bowl, cover with a damp cloth and let rise in a warm spot for 1 hour. Punch the dough down, cover and let rise another 30 minutes. Roll the dough out to a ¼ inch thickness. Line the bottom and sides of a buttered pie tin with the dough and prick with a fork. Cover with a damp cloth and let rise 30 minutes. Bake in a preheated 400° oven for 15 to 20 minutes or until golden brown. Remove the pastry from the pan and cool on a wire rack. Fill the pie with apricots, cherries or stewed fruits.

Pie from Limburg. The best known speciality of Limburg is the 'vlaai,' a pie filled with fruit. Businessmen from the North of Holland who have to go on business trips to Limburg always bring back a 'vlaai' for their wife and children. (recipe page 79, 4th column).

Hazelnoottaart

Hazelnut cake

 4 *eggs, separated*
 ¾ *cup sugar*
 1½ *cups ground hazelnuts*
 1 *cup self-rising flour*
 ⅔ *cup confectioners' sugar*
 1 *tablespoon water*
 ½ *teaspoon vanilla*
 ½ *cup hazelnuts*
   (filbert nuts)

Beat the egg yolks with ½ cup sugar until the mixture is very thick. Fold in the ground hazelnuts and flour. Beat the egg whites until soft peaks form. Add the remaining ¼ cup sugar and beat until stiff. Mix ⅓ of the egg whites into the batter until thoroughly combined. Fold in the remainder carefully. Place the batter, which will be quite stiff, in a well buttered and floured 8 inch spring form cake tin or other cake pan with 1½ inch sides. Bake in a preheated 350° oven for 40 to 45 minutes or until the cake tests done. Cool 5 minutes in the pan then remove to a wire rack. Mix together the confectioners' sugar, water and vanilla until smooth. Ice the top of the cake with the sugar mixture and decorate with hazelnuts.

Boules ardennaises

Ardenne balls

1 package dry yeast
¼ cup lukewarm water
1 (8 ounce) package cream
    cheese, softened
13 tablespoons butter, softened
2½ cups sifted all purpose flour
3 eggs, separated
Oil for deep frying
Powdered sugar

Sprinkle the yeast over the water and stir to dissolve. In the bowl of an electric mixer, beat the cream cheese and butter until smooth and fluffy. Add the flour and egg yolks alternately to make a thick batter. Beat the egg whites until stiff. Add the yeast mixture and ¼ of the egg whites to the flour mixture and combine thoroughly. Carefully fold in the remaining egg whites. Let the batter rise in a warm place for 30 minutes. Heat the oil for deep frying. Drop the batter by spoonfuls into the hot oil and fry 4 or 5 minutes or until the balls are puffy and brown. Drain on paper towels. Sprinkle with powdered sugar and serve.

Gâteau ardennais

Ardenne potato cake

½ pound potatoes
3 tablespoons flour
1 cup confectioners' sugar
3 eggs, separated

Boil the potatoes until tender. Drain and mash. Blend in the rice flour, confectioners' sugar and egg yolks until the ingredients are thoroughly combined. Beat the egg whites until stiff and carefully fold them into the potato mixture. Shape the mixture into a cone and place on a buttered baking sheet. Bake in a preheated 400° oven for 45 minutes to 1 hour. Serve cold with applesauce.

Kempense pruimetaartjes

Prune tarts from the Campine

2 tarts

For the pastry:
2 packages dry yeast
1 cup lukewarm milk
5 cups flour
½ teaspoon salt
6 tablespoons melted butter
½ cup sugar
½ teaspoon cinnamon
2 eggs, lightly beaten

For the filling:
½ pound dried pitted prunes,
    soaked overnight in water
    to cover
½ cup brown sugar
1 teaspoon cinnamon
1 egg, lightly beaten
2 tablespoons sugar

Prepare the pastry as described in the recipe for Pie from Limburg (page 84), adding the cinnamon when the butter is added. Let the dough rise as directed there. Cook the prunes, covered, in their soaking water with the brown sugar and cinnamon for 30 minutes or until tender. Drain and force the prunes through a sieve. Divide the pastry in half and roll each half out to a ¼ inch thickness. Line the bottom and sides of 2 buttered pie tins with the pastry and prick with a fork. Brush each tart with beaten egg and let stand 30 minutes. Spread the cakes with the prune mixture and sprinkle with sugar. Bake in a preheated 400° oven for 25 minutes. Cool the tarts on wire racks.

Appeltaart

Apple pie

2½ cups sifted all purpose flour
½ cup brown sugar
¼ teaspoon salt
10 tablespoons butter
1 egg yolk
  Grated rind of 1 lemon
1 pound cooking apples, peeled,
  cored and thinly sliced
¼ cup raisins
1 teaspoon cinnamon
¼ cup plus 2 tablespoons sugar
2 eggs
½ cup milk
2 tablespoons apricot jam

In a bowl, combine the flour, sugar and salt. Cut the butter into the flour mixture with a pastry blender or 2 knives until it resembles coarse meal. Add the egg yolk and lemon rind and knead the mixture together into a ball. Wrap in waxed paper and chill 1 hour. Roll the dough out on a floured board to a ¼ inch thickness. Line the bottom and sides of a buttered 9 inch pie or cake tin that has a removable bottom with the pastry. Arrange the apples and raisins on the pastry and sprinkle with the cinnamon and ¼ cup sugar. Beat the eggs with the milk and remaining sugar and pour over the apples. Bake the pie in a preheated 375° oven about 50 minutes. Let the pie cool in the tin. Unmold and spread the top of the pie with a thin layer of apricot jam. Serve with whipped cream.

Vlaamse wafels

Flemish waffles

4 to 6 servings

1 package dry yeast
2 cups lukewarm milk
4 eggs, separated
1 teaspoon vanilla
2 tablespoons brandy
2½ cups sifted all purpose flour
1 tablespoon powdered sugar
1 teaspoon salt
½ cup melted butter

Sprinkle the yeast over the lukewarm milk and stir to dissolve. Beat the egg yolks and add them to the yeast mixture with the vanilla and brandy. Sift together the flour, sugar and salt. Add the flour mixture to the liquid ingredients. Stir in the melted butter and combine thoroughly. Beat the egg whites until stiff and stir ¼ of the whites into the batter. Carefully fold in the remainder. Let the mixture stand in a warm place for about 45 minutes or until double in bulk. Heat a waffle iron and pour in about ½ cup of batter. Cook until done, about 8 minutes. Repeat until all the batter is used. Sprinkle the waffles with powdered sugar and serve as they come off the iron.

Overijse platte kaastaart

Cheese Cake from Overijse

For the pastry:
1 package dry yeast
½ cup lukewarm milk
2½ cups flour
½ teaspoon salt
3 tablespoons melted butter
2 tablespoons sugar
1 egg, lightly beaten

For the filling:
¼ cup applesauce
1 (8 ounce) package cream
  cheese
6 tablespoons sugar
2 eggs, separated
1 teaspoon vanilla
4 tablespoons crumbled
  macaroons
2 tablespoons finely chopped
  almonds
1 teaspoon dark rum

Prepare the pastry as described in the recipe for Pie from Limburg (page 84). Let the dough rise as directed in that recipe. Press the dough onto the bottom and sides of a buttered 10 inch cake tin. Spread the dough with a layer of applesauce. In the bowl of an electric mixer, beat the cream cheese until smooth and fluffy. Beat in the sugar, egg yolks and vanilla. Add the macaroons and almonds and combine thoroughly. Beat the egg whites until stiff and flavor with the rum. Stir ¼ of the egg whites into the cheese mixture and carefully fold in the remainder. Transfer the cheese mixture to the cake tin. Bake in a preheated 400° oven for 35 to 45 minutes or until golden brown. Chill before serving.

Dadelkoek

Date pie

10 tablespoons butter
1½ cups self-rising flour
1⅔ cups oatmeal
½ cup brown sugar
1 egg, lightly beaten
1 pound pitted dates

Beat the butter in a bowl until light and fluffy. Add the flour, oatmeal, brown sugar and egg and knead into a smooth dough. Chop the dates finely, reserving a few whole dates for garnish. Press half the dough into a well buttered 8 inch cake tin. Sprinkle with the chopped dates and cover with the remaining dough. Top with the reserved whole dates. Bake in a preheated 375° oven for about 1 hour. Let the "pie" cool in the tin. Serve with sherry flavored whipped cream.

Date pie (recipe page 83, 4th column)

Tough cake (recipe page 86, 4th column), Peppernuts (recipe page 87, 1st column) and Butter letter (recipe page 87, 2nd column)

Dutch doughnuts (recipe page 86, 2nd column)

85

Spicy cakes (recipe page 78, 2nd column)

December is a party month in Holland and Belgium, and everybody gains at least a few pounds during the festivities. The first major feast is St. Nicolaas night, celebrated in honor of the venerated bishop who comes from Spain on a ship each year, accompanied by his servant Black Peter and bringing toys and other presents for the children. At the end of November, the boat arrives in the harbor of Amsterdam, and St. Nicolaas is officially greeted by the mayor, often with many children and even the Royal family present. St. Nicolaas then mounts his white horse and rides through the streets of Amsterdam, the city of which he is patron saint. Thousands of children, accompanied by their parents, line the streets to cheer and call out 'Peeeete' so that Black Peter will hear and give them a generous handful of delicious peppernuts.

Up to the night of the 5th of December, St. Nicolaas rides his white horse over the rooftops and listens at the chimneys to hear if the children are singing songs in his honor. If they are, Black Peter drops toys and other presents down the chimneys right into the shoes the children have left out for this purpose. Often the children leave carrots in their shoes for St. Nicolaas' horse. Black Peter quickly descends the chimney, collects the carrot and then rejoins St. Nicolaas and the horse. Unfortunately, it is sometimes difficult to make

children believe this today when most of them live in apartment buildings with central heating. But the arrival of St. Nicolaas is still a much-awaited occasion in Holland, and even grown-ups secretly send each other gifts accompanied by long poems in which the small sins of the recipient are reproached. Piles and piles of cakes, 'speculaas', gingerbreads and marzipan are eaten at St. Nicolaas parties.

'Oliebollen' are a traditional treat on New Year's Eve in Holland. If they are fried too slowly the crusts become hard and tough and the doughnuts become greasy.

Kruidkoek

Oliebollen

Taai taai

Spicy cake

  2 *cups self-rising flour*
$\frac{1}{2}$ *cup dark brown sugar*
  1 *teaspoon ground cloves*
  1 *teaspoon cinnamon*
  1 *teaspoon powdered ginger*
$\frac{1}{2}$ *teaspoon grated nutmeg*
    Pinch of salt
$\frac{1}{3}$ *cup molasses*
  1 *cup milk*

Combine the dry ingredients in a bowl. Mix together the molasses and milk and add to the flour mixture, stirring until the batter is smooth. Place the batter in a well buttered and floured loaf pan and bake in a preheated 300° oven for about 1 hour or until the cake tests done. Leave the cake in the pan for 24 hours. This cake is served buttered at coffee time or at breakfast.

Dutch doughnuts

20 doughnuts

    1 *package dry yeast*
    1 *cup lukewarm milk*
 $2\frac{1}{4}$ *cups flour*
    2 *teaspoons salt*
    1 *egg, lightly beaten*
 $1\frac{1}{2}$ *cups mixed currants and raisins*
    1 *cooking apple, peeled, cored and chopped*
      Oil for deep frying
      Powdered sugar

Sprinkle the yeast over $\frac{1}{4}$ cup milk and stir to dissolve. Combine the flour and salt and add the remaining milk and the egg. Add the yeast mixture, currants, raisins and apple and mix well. Let stand in a warm place until doubled in bulk. Heat the oil for deep frying. Shape balls of the batter with two metal spoons and drop them into the hot fat a few at a time. Deep fry for 8 minutes or until golden brown. Drain on paper towels. Serve them piled on a dish and sprinkled with powdered sugar.

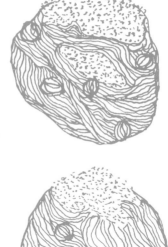

Tough cake

  3 *cups rye flour*
$1\frac{1}{2}$ *cups white flour*
$\frac{1}{2}$ *cup water*
$\frac{1}{2}$ *cup honey*
$\frac{1}{4}$ *cup molasses*
  1 *teaspoon powdered anise*
  1 *teaspoon ground cloves*
$1\frac{1}{2}$ *teaspoons cinnamon*
  1 *teaspoon ginger*
$1\frac{1}{2}$ *teaspoons baking soda*
$\frac{1}{2}$ *cup buttermilk*

Combine the rye and white flour in a large bowl. In a saucepan, bring the water, honey, molasses and anise to a boil and simmer 5 minutes. Add the liquid mixture to the flour and knead into a ball. Cover the dough and refrigerate for 2 days. Combine the cloves, cinnamon, ginger, baking soda and buttermilk and knead into the dough. Make sure the ingredients are well combined. Roll the dough out on a floured board to a $\frac{1}{2}$ inch thickness. Using cookie cutters, cut figures out of the dough. Place on buttered cookie sheets and brush with milk. Bake in a preheated 400° oven for 20 to 30 minutes.

On St. Nicholas day (December 5th) Black Peter, St. Nicholas' faithful helper, throws handfuls of peppernuts into the houses, while the children sing the well-known St. Nicholas songs, *suddenly the doorbell rings and a black-gloved hand (usually that of a friendly neighbor) throws the peppernuts through the opened door.*

Pepernoten

Peppernuts

1¼ cups flour
1¼ cups self-rising flour
½ cup brown sugar
1 egg yolk
2 tablespoons water
¼ teaspoon cinnamon
¼ teaspoon grated nutmeg
¼ teaspoon ground cloves
¼ teaspoon powdered anise
⅛ teaspoon salt

Knead all the ingredients together into a soft ball. Butter 2 baking sheets. Form about 90 marble-sized balls and place them on the baking sheets. Bake in a preheated 350° oven for about 20 minutes or until rather hard.

Boterletter

Butter letter

1 cup finely ground almonds
⅔ cup sugar
1 egg, lightly beaten
Grated rind of ½ lemon
1¼ cups flour
¼ teaspoon salt
½ cup (1 stick) butter
3 to 4 tablespoons ice water
1 egg yolk, lightly beaten

Combine the almonds, sugar, egg and lemon rind. Cover and let the mixture stand overnight. Place the flour and salt in a bowl. With a pastry blender or 2 knives, cut the butter into the flour until it resembles coarse meal. Add the water a little at a time, using only enough to make the mixture stick together. Wrap the dough in waxed paper and chill 1 hour. Roll the dough out on a floured board into a rectangle. Fold in thirds, wrap in waxed paper and refrigerate 15 minutes. Roll and fold the dough again and refrigerate. Repeat these steps 3 more times. After the last rolling and folding, refrigerate the dough 2 to 3 hours. Roll it into a long strip 4 inches wide and ⅛ inch thick. Make cylinders of the almond mixture 1 inch in diameter. Wrap a strip of dough around the almond mixture and press the dough together at the ends with wet fingers. Form the cylinders into letters and place on a buttered baking sheet. Brush with egg yolk and bake in a preheated 400° oven for 20 minutes or until golden brown. Cool on wire racks.

Appelflappen

Apple fritters

30 fritters

2½ cups flour
1¼ cups beer
¼ teaspoon salt
6 sour apples, peeled, cored
and sliced ½" thick
Oil for deep frying
Powdered sugar

Combine the flour, beer and salt and beat until smooth. Coat apple slices, a few at a time, with batter and deep fry them in the hot oil until light brown (3 to 4 minutes). Drain on paper towels and sprinkle with powdered sugar. Serve hot.

Kerstkransjes

Christmas rings

2 cups flour
¾ cup sugar
1 teaspoon baking powder
¼ teaspoon salt
Grated rind of ½ lemon
⅔ cup butter
1 tablespoon milk
1 egg, lightly beaten
Sugar
¼ cup chopped almonds

In a bowl, combine the flour, sugar, baking powder, salt and lemon rind. Cut the butter into the flour mixture with a pastry blender or 2 knives. Add the milk and knead the dough together into a ball. Wrap in waxed paper and refrigerate 1 hour. Roll out sections of the dough on a floured board to a ⅛ inch thickness. Cut rounds using a 2½ inch round cookie cutter. Cut out the center of the cookies using a thimble. Knead the centers back into the remaining dough. Place the rings on a buttered cookie sheet. Brush with beaten egg and sprinkle with sugar and almonds. Bake in a preheated 350° oven for 15 to 20 minutes or until golden brown. Let the rings cool on the baking sheet. Thread red ribbon through the holes and hang the cookies on the Christmas tree.

Decorated Christmas cake

Versierde Kerstkoek

Decorated Christmas cake

½ cup sugar
5 tablespoons honey
3 tablespoons melted butter
2 cups water
3¼ cups flour
1 teaspoon baking powder
½ teaspoon ground cloves
1 teaspoon cinnamon
1 teaspoon powdered anise
2 egg yolks, lightly beaten

In a bowl, combine the sugar, honey, butter and water and stir until well blended. Sift together the flour, baking powder, cloves, cinnamon and anise. Add the flour mixture gradually, mixing well after each addition. Cover the dough and let stand overnight. Roll the dough out on a lightly floured board to a ½ inch thickness. Cut various shapes with cookie cutters and outline the shapes with beaten egg yolk. Place the cakes on buttered cookie sheets and bake in a preheated 375° oven for 20 minutes or until golden brown. Decorate the cakes with tiny pieces of candied fruits, licorice or colored sprinkles.

The second major holiday in December is Christmas, and the celebration spreads over onto the 26th.
The last day of the year is also an important holiday. Restaurants, theaters and movies are closed and the streets are deserted. Indoors, the whole family gathers together on this day. Warm wine, New Years' Eve doughnuts and apple fritters are served, games are played with the children and at midnight supper is served, usually a herring or salmon salad. People in Holland believe you must eat the old year out and the new year in.

Beverages

Friese boerenkoffie

Coffee with beer Friesland style

6 servings

- 5 tablespoons butter
- 1¼ cups sugar
- 3 egg yolks
- 4 tablespoons flour
- 1 teaspoon cinnamon
- ½ teaspoon nutmeg
- 4 cups beer
- 1 cup brandy
- 1 cup hot, strong coffee

In the bowl of an electric mixer, beat the butter with the sugar, egg yolks, flour, cinnamon and nutmeg until light and fluffy. Beat in ½ cup of the beer. Bring the remaining beer to a boil and gradually pour it into the sugar mixture, beating constantly at the lowest speed. Transfer the mixture to a saucepan and heat over very low heat until almost boiling. Remove from the heat and stir in the brandy and hot coffee. Serve in large cups. This is a typical drink from northern Holland and is drunk during skating parties.

Slemp

Hot milk drink

6 servings

- 6 cloves
- ¼ teaspoon saffron threads
- 1 cinnamon stick
- 1 teaspoon tea leaves
- 1 teaspoon ground mace
- 6 cups milk
- ¼ cup sugar
- 3 tablespoons cornstarch dissolved in 3 tablespoons water

Tie the cloves, saffron threads, cinnamon stick and tea in a small piece of cheesecloth. Place the cheesecloth bag in a saucepan with the mace and milk. Bring the milk to a boil over low heat. Add the sugar and the cornstarch mixture, stirring constantly until the milk is slightly thickened. Remove the cheesecloth bag and pour the hot milk into mugs.

Kandeel

Hot white wine

6 servings

- 1 cup water
- 1 stick cinnamon
- 10 whole cloves
  Rind of 1 lemon, cut into strips
- 6 egg yolks
- ½ cup superfine sugar
- 1 full bottle dry white wine

Place the water, cinnamon, cloves and lemon rind in a small saucepan. Heat the mixture for 1 hour over the lowest possible heat. Strain and cool the liquid. Beat the egg yolks with the sugar until foamy. Stirring constantly, add the cooled liquid, then the wine. Place in a double boiler or very heavy pan and cook over low heat, stirring constantly until the mixture thickens. Do not allow it to boil. Serve hot in small cups.

Bisschop

Hot wine

8 to 10 servings

- 1 orange
- 20 cloves
- 4 small (½ inch) cinnamon sticks
- 2 bottles dry red wine
- ½ cup sugar
- 1 cup brandy (optional)

Wash the orange and spike it with the cloves and cinnamon sticks. Place it in a saucepan just large enough for all the ingredients. It must have a tight fitting lid. Add the wine and heat over very low heat for at least 2 hours. At no time should the wine be allowed to boil. If necessary, place the pan on an asbestos pad over the burner to prevent boiling. Before serving, remove the orange and stir in the sugar and optional brandy.

Chocolat à la luxembourgeoise

Chocolate Luxembourg style

6 servings

  5 *ounces semi-sweet chocolate*
  4 *cups milk*
  1 *teaspoon vanilla*
½ *cup heavy cream*
  1 *tablespoon sugar*
  2 *egg whites, stiffly beaten*

Combine the chocolate with ½ cup milk and stir over low heat until the chocolate is dissolved. Cook, stirring, for 3 to 4 minutes more. Add the remaining milk and heat, stirring constantly, until almost boiling. Stir in the vanilla and remove from the heat. Whip the cream with the sugar until stiff. Carefully fold the cream and egg whites together. Serve the chocolate in mugs topped with some of the whipped cream mixture.

Advocaat

Advocaat

10 to 12 servings

 10 *eggs*
 ½ *teaspoon salt*
1¼ *cups sugar*
  2 *cups brandy*
1½ *teaspoons vanilla*

In the bowl of an electric mixer, beat the eggs with the salt and sugar until very thick. Add the brandy slowly, beating constantly. Pour the mixture into a large, heavy saucepan or double boiler. Place the mixture over very low heat, beating constantly with a wire whisk until the advocaat is warm, not hot, and thickened. Remove from the heat and stir in the vanilla. Pour into a pitcher. Advocaat is served in a glass and eaten with a spoon. It is often served topped with whipped cream.

A traditional Dutch party drink is known as 'farmmaidens' (in center) and 'farm boys' (below right). Although it can now be bought ready-made, it is still made at home in many small villages. The drink of hot milk and spices is called 'slemp' (top right) in Dutch and it used to be served in Amsterdam at the municipal theater on New Year's Eve. According to tradition, the evening was devoted to a play about a famous event in the history of Amsterdam. Afterwards, the local authorities gave a reception and served 'slemp'. The reception is still given, but tastes have changed and wine is served instead of the Hot milk drink (recipe page 90, 2nd column). Hot beer (top left) and Advocaat (recipe page 91, 4th column) is shown below left.

Boerejongens

Farm boys

1 pound golden raisins
1¼ cups sugar
1 cup water
1 cinnamon stick
3½ cups sweet white wine
½ cup vodka

Wash the raisins in hot water and drain. Place the sugar and water in a saucepan and heat, stirring, until the sugar is dissolved. Add the cinnamon stick and raisins and cook over very low heat until the raisins are plump. Remove the raisins with a slotted spoon and place in a bottle with an air tight lid. Boil the liquid down for a few minutes until slightly thickened. Remove the cinnamon stick and pour the syrup over the raisins. Cool thoroughly, add the wine and vodka and seal the bottle. Let the drink mellow at least 3 months before serving. Serve in tall glasses and eat the raisins with a spoon.

Boeremeisjes

Farm maidens

1¾ cups sugar
1 cup water
Rind of 1 lemon, cut into strips
1 pound fresh apricots or
⅔ pound dried apricots
3½ cups sweet white wine
½ cup vodka

Place the sugar, water and lemon rind in a saucepan and heat, stirring, until the sugar dissolves. If fresh apricots are used, poach them in boiling water for 1 to 2 minutes, drain and remove the pits. Add them to the sugar-water mixture and let stand 24 hours. If dried apricots are used, cook them in boiling water for 10 minutes and drain. Add them to the sugar-water mixture and let stand 48 hours. Place the apricots in a bottle with a tight fitting lid. Remove the lemon rind from the liquid and pour it over the apricots. Add the wine and vodka and seal the bottle. Let the drink mellow 3 months before sampling.

Heet bier

Hot beer

6 servings

4 cups beer
2 cloves
2 cinnamon sticks
Rind of ½ lemon
2 eggs
⅔ cup brown sugar
½ cup rum
½ teaspoon salt

Heat the beer with the cloves, cinnamon sticks and lemon rind. Beat the eggs with the sugar until very thick. Gradually add the egg mixture to the hot beer, stirring constantly, until thoroughly blended. Do not allow the mixture to boil. Strain and discard the cloves, cinnamon sticks and lemon rind. Stir in the rum and salt and serve immediately.

Bière chaude

Belgian hot beer

6 servings

2 cups beer
2 cups sweet white wine
½ cup sugar
1 cinnamon stick
Rind of 1 lemon, cut into strips
4 egg yolks
½ cup warm milk
1 tablespoon cornstarch dissolved in
1½ tablespoons water

Place the beer, wine, sugar, cinnamon and lemon rind in a saucepan and heat slowly. In a small pan, beat the egg yolks into the warm milk and place over low heat. Add the cornstarch mixture and stir constantly until the mixture thickens. Do not allow it to boil. Add the egg yolk mixture to the heated beer, stirring constantly. Remove the pan from the heat. Discard the cinnamon stick and lemon rind and serve immediately.

Conversion tables

Liquid measures

American		metric equivalent
standard cup		(approximately)
1 cup = $\frac{1}{2}$ pint	= 8 fl. oz. (fluid ounce)	= 2,37 dl (deciliter)
1 tbs. (tablespoon)	= $\frac{1}{2}$ fl. oz.	= 1,5 cl (centiliter)
1 tsp. (teaspoon)	= $\frac{1}{6}$ fl. oz.	= 0,5 cl
1 pint	= 16 fl. oz.	= 4,73 dl
1 quart = 2 pints	= 32 fl. oz.	= 9,46 dl

British		metric equivalent
standard cup		(approximately)
1 cup = $\frac{1}{2}$ pint	= 10 fl. oz.	= 2,84 dl
1 tbs.	= 0.55 fl. oz.	= 1,7 cl
1 tsp.	= $\frac{1}{5}$ fl. oz.	= 0,6 cl
1 pint	= 20 fl. oz.	= 5,7 dl
1 quart = 2 pints	= 40 fl. oz.	= 1,1 l (liter)

1 cup = 16 tablespoons
1 tablespoon = 3 teaspoons

1 liter = 10 deciliter = 100 centiliter

Oven temperatures

Centigrade	Fahrenheit	
up to 105° C	up to 225° F	cool
105–135° C	225–275° F	very slow
135–160° C	275–325° F	slow
175–190° C	350–375° F	moderate
215–230° C	400–450° F	hot
230–260° C	450–500° F	very hot
260° C	500° F	extremely hot

Solid measures

American/British		metric equivalent
		(approximately)
1 lb. (pound)	= 16 oz. (ounces)	= 453 g (gram)
	1 oz.	= 28 g
2.2 lbs.		= 1000 g = 1 kg (kilogram)
	$3\frac{1}{2}$ oz.	= 100 g

Kitchen terms

Aspic
A stiff gelatine obtained by combining fish or meat bouillon with gelatine powder.

Au gratin
Obtained by covering a dish with a white sauce (usually prepared with grated cheese) and then heating the dish in the oven so that a golden crust forms.

Baste
To moisten meat or other foods while cooking to add flavor and to prevent drying of the surface. The liquid is usually melted fat, meat drippings, fruit juice or sauce.

Blanch (precook)
To preheat in boiling water or steam. (1) Used to inactivate enzymes and shrink food for canning, freezing and drying. Vegetables are blanched in boiling water or steam, and fruits in boiling fruit juice, syrup, water or steam. (2) Used to aid in removal of skins from nuts, fruits and some vegetables.

Blend
To mix thoroughly two or more ingredients.

Fold
To combine by using two motions, cutting vertically through the mixture and turning over and over by sliding the implement across the bottom of the mixing bowl with each turn.

Fry
To cook in fat; applied especially (1) to cooking in a small amount of fat, also called sauté or pan-fry; (2) to cooking in a deep layer of fat, also called deep-fat frying.

Marinate
To let food stand in a marinade usually an oil–acid mixture like French dressing.

Parboil
To boil until partially cooked. The cooking is usually completed by another method.

Poach
To cook in a hot liquid using precautions to retain shape. The temperature used varies with the food.

Roast
To cook, uncovered, by dry heat. Usually done in an oven, but occasionally in ashes, under coals or on heated stones or metals. The term is usually applied to meats but may refer to other food as potatoes, corn, chestnuts.

Sauté
To brown or cook in a small amount of fat. See Fry.

Simmer
To cook in a liquid just below the boiling point, at temperatures of 185°–210° Bubbles form slowly and collapse below the surface.

Alphabetical index

Index by type of dish

photo credits
Bob Ris, Studio Meijer Pers, B.V., Amsterdam: pp. 4, 5 (top left), 8 (farmers), 9 (below), 16, 17, 20, 21, 24 (top), 32, 33, 45, 48, 52 (below), 53, 69 (below), 72, 73, 77, 80, 81, 84, 88, 89, 92
Ed Suister, Amsterdam: pp. 24 (below), 36, 37, 49 (top), 69 (below)
Henk van der Heijden, Amsterdam: pp. 41, 44
Peter van der Velde, Amsterdam: pp. 12, 13 (right)
Dolf Kruger p. 5 (right)
Belgian Touring Agency: p. 13 (left)
Spaarnestad NV, Haarlem: pp. 5 (below), 25, 28, 29, 40, 49 (below), 52 (top), 69 (top), 76, 85
VVV Alcmaria, Alkmaar: p. 8 (below)
VVV The Hague, The Hague: p. 9 (top)

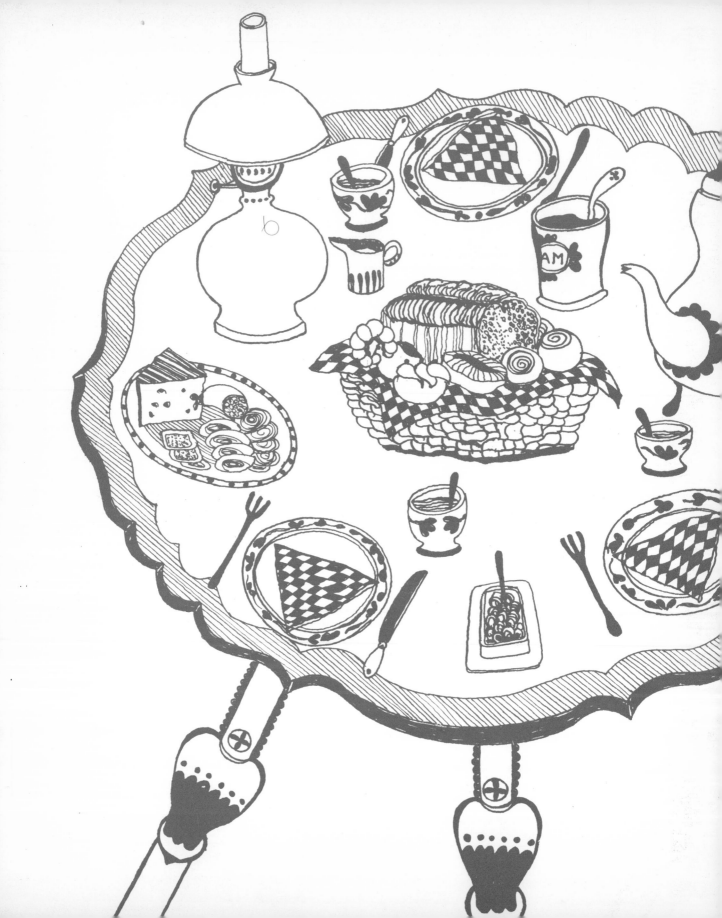